Pagan Portals
&
Shaman Pathways

...an ever-growing library of shared knowledge.

Moon Books has created two unique series where leading authors
and practitioners come together to share their knowledge,
passion and expertise across the complete Pagan spectrum. If you
would like to contribute to either series, our proposal procedure
is simple and quick, just visit our website (www.MoonBooks.net)
and click on Author Inquiry to begin the process.

If you are a reader with a comment about a book or a suggestion
for a title we'd love to hear from you! You can find us at
facebook.com/MoonBooks or you can keep up to date with new
releases etc on our dedicated Portals page at facebook.com/
paganportalsandshamanpathways/

*'Moon Books has achieved that rare feat of being synonymous with top-
quality authorship AND being endlessly innovative and exciting.'*
Kate Large, Pagan Dawn

Pagan Portals

Animal Magic, Rachel Patterson
An introduction to the world of animal magic and working with animal spirit guides

Australian Druidry, Julie Brett
Connect with the magic of the southern land, its seasons, animals, plants and spirits

Blacksmith Gods, Pete Jennings
Exploring dark folk tales and customs alongside the magic and myths of the blacksmith Gods through time and place

Brigid, Morgan Daimler
Meeting the Celtic Goddess of Poetry, Forge, and Healing Well

By Spellbook & Candle, Mélusine Draco
Why go to the bother of cursing, when a bottling or binding can be just as effective?

By Wolfsbane & Mandrake Root, Mélusine Draco
A study of poisonous plants, many of which have beneficial uses in both domestic medicine and magic

Candle Magic, Lucya Starza
Using candles in simple spells, seasonal rituals and essential craft techniques

Celtic Witchcraft, Mabh Savage
Wield winds of wyrd, dive into pools of wisdom; walk side by side with the Tuatha Dé Danann

Herbs of the Sun, Moon and Planets, Steve Andrews
The planets that rule over herbs that grow on Earth

Hoodoo, Rachel Patterson
Learn about and experience the fascinating magical art of
Hoodoo

Irish Paganism, Morgan Daimler
Reconstructing the beliefs and practices of pre-Christian Irish
Paganism for the modern world

Kitchen Witchcraft, Rachel Patterson
Take a glimpse at the workings of a Kitchen Witch and share in
the crafts

Meditation, Rachel Patterson
An introduction to the beautiful world of meditation

Merlin: Once and Future Wizard, Elen Sentier
Merlin in history, Merlin in mythology, Merlin through the ages
and his continuing relevance

Moon Magic, Rachel Patterson
An introduction to working with the phases of the Moon

Nature Mystics, Rebecca Beattie
Tracing the literary origins of modern Paganism

Pan, Mélusine Draco
An historical, mythological and magical insight into the God Pan

Pathworking through Poetry, Fiona Tinker
Discover the esoteric knowledge in the works of Yeats, O'Sullivan
and other poets

Runes, Kylie Holmes
The Runes are a set of 24 symbols that are steeped in history, myths and legends. This book offers practical and accessible information for anyone to understand this ancient form of divination

Sacred Sex and Magick, Web PATH Center
Wrap up ecstasy in love to create powerful magick, spells and healing

Spirituality without Structure, Nimue Brown
The only meaningful spiritual journey is the one you consciously undertake

The Awen Alone, Joanna van der Hoeven
An introductory guide for the solitary Druid

The Cailleach, Rachel Patterson
Goddess of the ancestors, wisdom that comes with age, the weather, time, shape-shifting and winter

The Morrigan, Morgan Daimler
On shadowed wings and in raven's call, meet the ancient Irish Goddess of war, battle, prophecy, death, sovereignty, and magic

Urban Ovate, Brendan Howlin
Simple, accessible techniques to bring Druidry to the wider public

Your Faery Magic, Halo Quin
Tap into your Natural Magic and become the Fey you are

Zen Druidry, Joanna van der Hoeven
Zen teachings and Druidry combine to create a peaceful life path that is completely dedicated to the here and now

Shaman Pathways

Aubry's Dog, Melusine Draco
A practical and essential guide to using canine magical energies

Black Horse White Horse, Mélusine Draco
Feel the power and freedom as Black Horse, White Horse guides you down the magical path of this most noble animal

Celtic Chakras, Elen Sentier
Tread the British native shaman's path, explore the Goddess hidden in the ancient stories; walk the Celtic chakra spiral labyrinth

Druid Shaman, Danu Forest
A practical guide to Celtic shamanism with exercises and techniques as well as traditional lore for exploring the Celtic Otherworld

Elen of the Ways, Elen Sentier
British shamanism has largely been forgotten: the reindeer Goddess of the ancient Boreal forest is shrouded in mystery... follow her deer-trods to rediscover her old ways

Following the Deer Trods, Elen Sentier
A practical handbook for anyone wanting to begin the old British paths. Follows on from Elen of the Ways

Trees of the Goddess, Elen Sentier
Work with the trees of the Goddess and the old ways of Britain

Way of the Faery Shaman, Flavia Kate Peters
Your practical insight into Faeries and the elements they engage
to unlock real magic that is waiting to help you

Web of Life, Yvonne Ryves
A new approach to using ancient ways in these contemporary
and often challenging times to weave your life path

What people are saying about

Have a Cool Yule

As per usual and in great style, Mélusine Draco presents a wealth of information about this historically proven pagan festival. Whichever way the reader chooses to celebrate...whether it's a traditional family Christmas or a traditional Yule in the company of pagan friends or as a solitary – there is something for everyone. From a complete festival calendar with some simple rites and symbolism, to carol lyrics, recipes, gift ideas and feasting to the 'art of using up' and festive games; everything Yuletide is covered. And with generous doses of light-hearted good cheer and a sprinkling of dark humour, the author strikes a balance that is both useful, informative and entertaining. A charming little book.
Sheena Cundy, Witch Lit author *The Madness and the Magic*

This certainly makes a cool yule for me! So much information, such fun too. It puts a whole new slant on our perhaps limited ideas of yuletide. And love the cover with the triumphant hare mounted on a dog...turns all preconceptions upside-down. Do read, you'll enjoy.
Elen Sentier, author of *Merlin: The Once and Future Wizard*, *Elen of the Ways* and *The Celtic Chakras*.

Have a Cool Yule is a lovely guide on how to truly enjoy the festive season in the depths of winter, whether you call it Christmas, the Winter Solstice, Yule or any other name. In the pages of this book you will find time-honoured traditions, recipes and sensible advice on how to avoid the worst of the commercialism and make the occasion what you want it to be.
Lucya Starza, author of *Pagan Portals – Candle Magic*

Pagan Portals

Have a Cool Yule

How-To Survive (and Enjoy) the
Mid-Winter Festival

Pagan Portals
Have a Cool Yule

How-To Survive (and Enjoy) the
Mid-Winter Festival

Mélusine Draco

Winchester, UK
Washington, USA

First published by Moon Books, 2017
Moon Books is an imprint of John Hunt Publishing Ltd., Laurel House, Station Approach,
Alresford, Hants, SO24 9JH, UK
office1@jhpbooks.net
www.johnhuntpublishing.com
www.moon-books.net

For distributor details and how to order please visit the 'Ordering' section on our website.

Text copyright: Mélusine Draco 2017

ISBN: 978 1 78535 711 4
978 1 78535 712 1 (ebook)
Library of Congress Control Number: 2017939487

A CIP catalogue record for this book is available from the British Library.

Design: Stuart Davies

Printed and bound by CPI Group (UK) Ltd, Croydon, CR0 4YY, UK

We operate a distinctive and ethical publishing philosophy in
all areas of our business, from our global network of authors to
production and worldwide distribution.

Contents

Chapter One

A Bit of Background Detail

Towards the end of the year the internet is full of pagan postings bemoaning the fact that they *hate* Christmas. How all the pagan meaning has been profaned and announcing that they will be holed up in solitary misery until all the commercially decadent festivities are over – all of which sadly demonstrates a complete lack of awareness concerning our pagan ancestry and its customs. Let's understand one thing before we go further: the Church did *not* invent the Mid-Winter Festival…it was there with all its rich pageantry of feasting and celebration long before Pope Julius I officially decreed, in the 4th century AD, that the birth of Jesus would henceforth be celebrated on the 25th December.

There are several factors that may have influenced this choice. December 25th was the date the Romans marked as the *Dies Natalis Solis Invicti* (the birth of the Unconquered Sun), which was easily massaged to become the 'Unconquered Son' based on some obscure Old Testament verse (Malachi 4:2) where the Messiah was identified with the sun. The date was exactly nine months following Annunciation, when the conception of Jesus was celebrated in the Christian calendar. Biblical scholars, however, reckon it most likely Jesus was born late August or September, because 'when John leapt in Elizabeth's womb at the presence of Jesus in Mary' it was during the Festival of Lights (Chanukah) in December and that is more likely closer to his *conception* than birth!

More importantly, it was also around the birth date of Mithras, whose following rivalled that of early Christianity; although Mithraic iconography always portrays Mithras and the sun god as separate beings, in Mithraic inscriptions this god of the Roman Legions was often identified with the sun by being called 'Sol Invictus' – the Unconquered Sun. Finally, the Romans also celebrated a series of pagan solstice festivals near the end of the year, so the calendar dates were realigned to appropriate these sacred days for the Christian holy days, but without any historical evidence to justify this hijacking of pagan customs.

'But there's nothing here for us to celebrate,' some lonely pagans cry.

Au contraire, mes amies!

Professor E O James, an anthropologist in the field of comparative religion writing in *Seasonal Feasts and Festivals*, had this to offer:

> From time immemorial the turn of the year in mid-winter had been the occasion of rites of passage as a precaution against supernatural forces thought to be rampant, and to ensure the renewal of the waning power of the sun… Therefore, the Church was confronted with a very firmly established and highly developed calendrical ritual, though it was not until towards the end of the fourth century that it was associated with the birth of Christ.

In *Rites and Symbols on Initiation*, Professor Mircea Eliade, a leading scholar of religion, also comments on the Germanic 'fundamental experience provoked by the initiates' meeting with the dead, who return to Earth more especially about the Winter Solstice'. She continued: 'In other words, during the winter the members of the band are able to transmute their profane condition and attain superhuman existence, whether by consorting with the Ancestors or by appropriating the behaviour that is the *magic* of the carnivora.'

This, these academic sources tell us, Winter Solstice or **Mid-Winter Festival** as our ancestors would have called it, is the most magical and mystical time of the year and should be celebrated as such with all the pagan gusto we can summon. It is an ancient fire festival that heralds the shortest day of the year; an astronomical turning of the tide to announce the rebirth of the sun and the promise of warmth returning to the land. It was a time of long nights and short days. It was cold and dark and not a time to be venturing out. It was, therefore, the perfect time to feast and create artificial light and warmth – and look forward with hope to the return of the sun.

In those far-off days, the British winter was more severe than now, but the Winter Solstice would have been a special moment during the year even in Neolithic times. This is confirmed by the layouts of those great late Neolithic and Bronze Age archaeological sites, such as Stonehenge in England, Maeshowe in the Orkneys and Newgrange in Ireland. The primary axes of these ancient monuments were carefully aligned with the Winter Solstice sunrise (Newgrange) and the Winter Solstice sunset (Stonehenge and Maeshowe); Stonehenge's Great Trilithon was erected facing outwards from the middle of the monument, with its smooth flat face turned towards the mid-winter sun. The Winter Solstice was immensely important because these ancient people were economically dependent on monitoring the progress of the seasons.

The reasons for this are obvious – and demonstrate why the Mid-Winter Festival with all its trappings of feasting and plenty should remain one of the most important feasts in the pagan calendar – if only as a testament to those who didn't make it through the long winter darkness. Starvation was common during the long months of winter, which were also known as 'the famine months'. The old Mid-Winter Festival according to the calendar re-alignment now falls on 6th January, which the Anglo-Saxons called *Wolfmonath*, when wolves moved closer to human habitation to feed off the carcases of fallen stock. The festival was the last opportunity for feasting, before deep winter began; when a large proportion of the cattle were slaughtered so they would not have to be fed during the winter, and it was the only time of year when a plentiful supply of fresh meat was available. The majority of wine and beer made during the year was finally fermented and also ready for drinking at this time.

If we look at traditional Christmas cards and paintings from medieval times onwards, everywhere is covered in deep snow, and 'frost fairs' were even held on the frozen Thames at London. One of the earliest accounts comes from 250AD, when it was frozen solid for six weeks. As long ago as 923AD the river was even open to wheeled traffic for trade and the transport of goods for thirteen weeks; in 1410, the ice lasted for fourteen weeks. During the Great Frost of 1683-84, the worst frost recorded in England, the Thames was completely frozen for two months, with the ice reaching a thickness of eleven inches at London.

When the ice was thick enough and lasted long enough, Londoners would take to the river for travel, trade and entertainment, the latter eventually taking the form of public festivals and fairs. The Thames had frozen over several times in the 16th century – Henry VIII travelled from central London to Greenwich by sleigh along the river in 1536; Elizabeth I took to the ice frequently during 1564, to 'shoot at marks', and small boys played football on the ice. The first recorded frost fair was in 1608 and the most celebrated occurred in the winter of 1683-84 and was described by John Evelyn:

Coaches plied from Westminster to the Temple, and from several other stairs to and fro, as in the streets; sleds, sliding with skeetes, a bull-baiting, horse and coach races, puppet plays and interludes, cooks, tipling and other lewd places, so that it seemed to be a bacchanalian triumph, or carnival on the water. For sixpence, the printer Croom sold souvenir cards written with the customer's name, the date, and the fact that the card was printed on the Thames, and was making five pounds a day (ten times a labourer's weekly wage). King Charles II bought one.

The cold weather was not only a cause for merriment, as Evelyn explained. There were tragedies, too:

> The fowls, fish and birds, and all our exotic plants and greens universally perishing. Many parks of deer were destroyed, and all sorts of fuel so dear that there were great contributions to keep the poor alive... London, by reason for the excessive coldness of the air hindering the ascent of the smoke, was so filled with the fuliginous steam of the sea-coal... that one could hardly breathe...

Thames frost fairs were often brief, and scarcely commenced before the weather lifted, causing people to retreat from the melting ice. Rapid thaws sometimes caused loss of life and property. In January 1789, melting ice dragged a ship that was anchored to a riverside public house, pulling the building down and causing five people to be crushed to death.

This period from the mid-14th century to the 19th century in Europe is known as the Little Ice Age because of the severity of the climate, especially the winters. Snowfall was much heavier and lay on the ground for many months longer than it does today, but the Mid-Winter Festival meant that the longest night had passed and the weather would eventually improve. Anyone whose roots dig deep into the North-European gene-pool will be linked to ancestors for whom the Winter Solstice was probably the most important observance of the year after the Harvest Festival. So can modern pagans really claim that this time of the year means nothing to them?

Needless to say, Roman, Celt, Anglo-Saxon and Norse invaders also brought their Mid-Winter customs with them, and as they integrated with the native peoples, so these customs were melded into existing ones. The concentration of these observances were not always on the day commencing at midnight or at dawn, but at the beginning of the pagan day, which in many cultures fell on the previous Eve.

The Romans would have brought **Saturnalia** to Britain, an ancient festival held in honour of Saturn, held on 17th December of the Julian calendar and later expanded with festivities through to 23rd. The 17th December was the first day of the astrological sign of Capricorn, the house of Saturn, the planet named for the god and its proximity to the Winter Solstice was endowed with a wide range of mystical meanings. The holiday was celebrated with a sacrifice at the Temple of Saturn in the Roman Forum with a public banquet, followed by private gift-giving, continual partying, and a carnival atmosphere that overturned Roman social norms: gambling was permitted and masters provided table service for their slaves – echoing the later medieval English custom of the Lord of Misrule. The poet Catullus called it 'the best of days'.

Although probably the best-known Roman holiday, Saturnalia is not fully described in any single historical source and our information is pieced together from several accounts dealing with various aspects of the celebrations. In an extract from classical writer, Macrobius's work, Saturnalia is a festival of light leading up to the Winter Solstice, 'with the abundant presence of candles symbolising the quest for knowledge and truth'. The popularity of Saturnalia continued into the 3rd and 4th centuries AD and, as the empire came under Christian rule, many of its customs influenced the later seasonal celebrations surrounding the Christmas observances.

Saturnalia is best known for its role reversal and behavioural license when slaves were treated to a banquet of the kind usually enjoyed by their masters; and there are hints of mask-wearing or '*guising*'. Gambling and dice-playing, normally prohibited or at least frowned upon, were permitted for all, even slaves, where coins and nuts were the stakes. Rampant overeating and drunkenness became the rule, and a sober person was the exception. Wikipedia quotes Seneca, who looked forward to the holiday, if somewhat tentatively, in a letter to a friend:

It is now the month of December, when the greatest part of the city is in a bustle. Loose reins are given to public dissipation; everywhere you may hear the sound of great preparations, as if there were some real difference between the days devoted to Saturn and those for transacting business... Were you here, I would willingly confer with you as to the plan of our conduct; whether we should eve in our usual way, or, to avoid singularity, both take a better supper and throw off the toga.

Some Romans found it all a bit too much for them and Pliny described a secluded suite of rooms in his Laurentine villa, to which he used to retreat: '...especially during the Saturnalia when the rest of the house is noisy with the licence of the holiday and festive cries. This way I don't hamper the games of my people and they don't hinder my work or studies.'

The Romans were also great gift-givers and the **Sigillaria** on 19th December was a special day of exchanging presents. Because gifts of value would suggest a social status contrary to the spirit of the season, these were often the pottery or wax figurines called *sigillaria* made especially for the day: candles, or 'gag gifts', novelties, of which the Emperor Augustus was particularly fond (he would have loved modern pound-shops!), while children received toys as gifts.

In his many poems about the Saturnalia, Martial names both expensive and quite cheap gifts, including writing tablets, dice, knucklebones, moneyboxes, combs, toothpicks, a hat, a hunting knife, an axe, various lamps, balls, perfumes, pipes, a pig, a sausage, a parrot, tables, cups, spoons, items of clothing, statues, masks, books, and pets. Gifts might be as costly as a slave or exotic animal, but Martial suggests that token gifts of low intrinsic value inversely measure the high quality of a friendship. Patrons might pass along a gratuity *(sigillaricium)* to their poorer clients or dependents to help them buy gifts. There was also a Roman practice of a verse accompanying a gift that could possibly be the forerunner of the modern custom of sending greeting cards.

Sol Invictus ('The Unconquered Sun') was originally a Syrian god who was later adopted as the chief god of the Roman Empire under Emperor Aurelian. His holiday was traditionally celebrated on December 25th, as are several gods associated with the Winter Solstice in many pagan traditions, including Mithras, that popular god of the Roman Legions, whose festival, **Yalda**, was celebrated on 21st December. Several Mithraic temples have been discovered in Britain and so the celebrations would have been known to those Romano-British who lived in close proximity to them.

The pagan Scandinavian and Germanic people of northern Europe celebrated a twelve-day mid-winter holiday called **Yule** and more modern Christmas traditions, such as the festive tree, wreath, and log, are direct descendants of those old Yuletide customs. Scandinavians still call Yule *Jul,* but in English from around 900AD, the word was often used in combination with the season: Yuletide. A *'julblot'* was the most solemn sacrificial feast that was given to the gods to earn blessing on the forthcoming germinating crops.

Yule is the modern representation of the Old English words *ġéol* and *ġéola,* with the former indicating the twelve-day festival of Yule, and the latter indicating the month of Yule, whereby *ǽrra ġéola* referred to the period before the Yule festival (December) and *æftera ġéola* referred to the period after Yule (January). The traditional Twelve Days of Christmas, also known as 'Twelvetide', is now recognised as running from Christmas Day with the Twelve Days being 25th December to 5th January. Or starting with the Anglo-Saxon **Modraniht** (Mother's Night) on 24th – the beginning of the 'Time between the Years' – the thirteen sacred days and twelve sacred nights.

In medieval and Tudor England, the **Twelfth Night** marked the end of a winter festival that started on All Hallows Eve! At the beginning of the Twelfth Night festival, a cake that contained a bean was shared and the person who found the bean would rule the feast. Midnight signalled the end of his rule and the world would return to normal. The common theme was that the normal order of things was reversed. This tradition dates back to pre-Christian European festivals such as the Celtic festival of Samhain and the Roman Saturnalia. Food and drink were an important part of the celebrations and many of the traditional recipes go back many centuries. A punch called *wassail* was consumed especially on Twelfth Night and throughout the whole holiday, particularly in Britain. Around the world, special pastries, such as the tortell and king cake, were baked on Twelfth Night and eaten the following day.

While mostly considered to be a British mid-winter custom, the appointment of a Lord of Misrule comes from the ancient Roman feast of Saturnalia. During this time the ordinary rules of life were subverted as masters served their slaves, and the offices of state were held by slaves. The Lord of Misrule presided over all of this, and had the power to command anyone to do anything during the holiday period. In the Tudor period, the Lord of Misrule is mentioned a number of times in contemporary documents referring to revels both at court and among the ordinary people. John Stow in his *Survey of London*, published in 1603, gives a description of the Lord of Misrule:

[I]n the feaste of Christmas, there was in the kinges house, wheresoeuer hee was lodged, a Lord of Misrule, or Maister of merry disports, and the like had yee in the house of euery noble man, of honor, or good worshippe, were he spirituall or temporall. Amongst the which the Mayor of London, and eyther of the shiriffes had their seuerall Lordes of Misrule, euer contending without quarrell or offence, who should make the rarest pastimes to delight the Beholders. These Lordes beginning their rule on Alhollon Eue [Halloween], continued the same till the morrow after the Feast of the Purification, commonlie called Candlemas day: In all which space there were fine and subtle disguisinges, Maskes and Mummeries, with playing at Cardes for Counters, Nayles and pointes in euery house, more for pastimes then for gaine.

According to the anthropologist James Frazer in *The Golden Bough*, however, there was a darker side to the celebrations. Roman soldiers would choose a man from among them to be the Lord of Misrule for thirty days. At the end of that period, his throat was cut on the altar of Saturn. Similar origins of the British Lord of Misrule as a sacrificial king (a *temporary king*, as Frazer puts it) who was later put to death for the benefit of all, have also been recorded. While the medieval and later Roman custom of a Lord of Misrule as a master of revels – a figure of fun and no more than that – is more familiar, there does seem to be some indication of an earlier and darker aspect to this rite.

The Lord of Misrule is also referred to by Philip Stubbes in his *Anatomie of Abuses* (1585) where he states that 'the wilde heades of the parishe conventynge together, chuse them a grand Capitaine (of mischeefe) whom they ennobel with the title Lorde of Misrule'. He then gives a description of the way they dress colourfully, tie bells onto their legs and 'go to the churche (though the minister be at praier or preachyng) dauncying and swingyng their handercheefe' reminiscent of the Morris dances still performed today.

The mid-winter tradition of **Wassailing** also falls into two distinct categories: the house-visiting wassail and the orchard-visiting wassail. The house-visiting wassail is the practice of people going door-to-door, singing and offering a drink from the wassail bowl in exchange for gifts. This practice still exists in some parts, but has largely been displaced by carol-singers. The orchard-visiting wassail refers to the ancient custom of visiting orchards in cider-producing regions of England, reciting incantations and singing to the trees to promote a good harvest for the coming year'

The word *wassail* comes from the Anglo-Saxon greeting Wæs þu hæl, meaning 'be thou hale', i.e., 'be in good health'. The correct response to the greeting is *Drinc hæl*. According to the *Oxford English Dictionary, waes hael* is the Middle English (and hence post-Norman) spelling parallel to OE *hál wes þú*, and was a greeting not a toast, 'Neither in Old English nor in Old Norse, nor indeed in any Germanic language, has any trace been found of the use as drinking formulas.' Later, in the 12th century, Danish-speaking inhabitants of England turned 'was hail', and the reply 'drink hail', into a drinking formula, a toast widely adopted by the indigenous population of England. So, now you know!

We also must remember that within the early Church many of the traditions and customs practised on 'holy' days can be traced back to pre-Christian times when specific events were endowed with magical or spiritual attributes that were incorporated into festivals and celebrations. These customs were so firmly entrenched in the hearts and minds of the people, that when Christianity was finding a foothold in Britain, the Church of Rome integrated and sanctified them. The Church slowly drew the people in by allowing the old festivals to continue with a veneer of Christianity overlaid upon them, with Anglo-Saxon, Norman and early medieval churches being decorated with festive mid-winter greenery (which was later banned as being pagan).

And as for those horrendous renderings of Christmas carols usually encountered blaring out in supermarkets and shopping malls that drive us barmy from mid-November onwards... well, almost all the well-known carols were not sung in church until the second half of the 19th century. According to *Encyclopædia Britannica*, 19th century antiquarians rediscovered about 500 early carols in various museums. Some are wassailing songs, some are religious songs in English, some are in Latin, and some are 'macaronic' – a mixture of Old English and Latin – the most famous survival being *The Boar's Head*.

The Boar's Head carol is of 15th century origin and describes the ancient tradition of sacrificing a boar and presenting its head at a Yuletide feast. Of the several extant versions of the carol, the one most usually performed today, is based on a version published in 1521 in Wynkyn de Worde's *Christmasse Carolles*. According to folklorists, the boar's head tradition was '...initiated in all probability on the Isle of Britain by the Anglo-Saxons, although our knowledge of it comes substantially from medieval times... [In ancient Norse tradition] sacrifice carried the intent of imploring Freyr to show favor to the New Year. The boar's head with apple in mouth was carried into the banquet hall on a gold or silver dish to the sounds of trumpets and the songs of minstrels.'

The boar's head in hand bring I, [Or: *The boar's head in hand bear I,*]
Bedeck'd with bays and rosemary.
And I pray you, my masters, be merry [Or: *And I pray you, my masters, merry be*]
Quot estis in convivio [Translation: *As many as are in the feast*]

Chorus
Caput apri defero [Translation: *The boar's head I offer*]
Reddens laudes Domino [Translation: *Giving praises to the Lord*]

The boar's head, as I understand,
Is the rarest dish in all this land,
Which thus bedeck'd with a gay garland
Let us servire cantico. [Translation: *Let us serve with a song*]

In Scandinavia and England, Saint Stephen may have inherited some of Freyr's legacy. St Stephen's feast day is 26th December (Boxing Day), and so he came to play a part in the Yuletide celebrations that were previously associated with Freyr (or *Ingwi* to the Anglo-Saxons). In old Swedish art, Stephen is shown as tending to horses and bringing a boar's head to a Yuletide banquet. Both elements may be pagan survivals and the traditional Christmas ham may have originated as a Winter Solstice boar sacrifice to Freyr.

The Holly and the Ivy – the symbolism of this anonymous early carol relates to ancient fertility mythology and the association of the male with holly and good and the female with ivy and evil. Surprisingly, the ivy is never mentioned after the first line, which suggests there are some lost verses, or that the carol has been extensively re-written.

The holly and the ivy,
When they are both full grown,
Of all the trees that are in the wood,
The holly bears the crown.

Refrain
O the rising of the sun
And the running of the deer,
The playing of the merry organ,
Sweet singing in the choir.

Similarly, the carol *In the Bleak Midwinter* refers to the Winter Solstice in its title despite being based on a contemporary poem by the English poet Christina Rossetti, written before 1872 and published posthumously in 1904.

In the bleak mid-winter
Frosty wind made moan,
Earth stood hard as iron,
Water like a stone;
Snow had fallen, snow on snow,
Snow on snow,
In the bleak mid-winter
Long ago.

As we can see, we only have to scratch the thin veneer of 'Christmas' to find a highly important pagan holiday with the majority of its ancient traditions preserved intact. Strangely, the ubiquitous pagan

'Wheel of the Year' now assigns the Winter Solstice to the place of a minor *sabbat*, and yet as we've discovered, it was probably *the* most sacred festival of the year for our pagan ancestors. Nevertheless, these associations reveal that the Mid-Winter Festival was a time of magic and mystery for the ancient Britons, the Germanic tribes and the migratory Celts and Anglo-Saxons, as well as a time for feasting and celebration.

It doesn't matter where we live in the New or Old World, it would be a pity to ignore these facts and not celebrate the season with mirth and merriment as our forebears did – and not let Christian hype and gross commercialism ruin the true magic of the Winter Solstice. Perhaps it's time to embrace the pagan sacredness of the Mid-Winter Festival and reclaim that which was taken from us by the most insidious of means – absorption!

After all… what *is* there for anyone who calls themselves 'pagan' to hate about ancient pagan traditions?

Chapter Two

The 32 Days of Yuletide

It is unwise to lay down the law over the exact number of days required to celebrate the pagan Mid-Winter Festival, but needless to say it renders the seasonal song *The Twelve Days of Christmas* redundant. By the time the pagan romancer had reached *'On the thirty-second day of Yuletide my true love sent to me...'* the recipient would probably have either a) gone mad, b) throttled the delivery man, or c) had the gift-bearing true love charged with harassment. Our celebrations (or observances) might last for a whole month, but it doesn't mean maxing out the credit card or applying for a bank loan; it *doesn't* have to cost a fortune and if friends and family don't like more modest gifts... tough! Remember the poet Martial suggestion that 'token gifts of low intrinsic value inversely measure the high quality of a friendship'.

On the other hand, just because *we've* opted out of a traditional Christmas with all the trimmings, doesn't mean to say we have to be churlish about it. There is little point in making a stand over one day of the year, which will escalate into a major family feud taking until Easter to sort out. Yes, I appreciate the brother-in-law eats with his mouth open; your elder brother's children are usually throwing up by mid-afternoon; your OCD sister has hysterics in the downstairs cloakroom because there are only paper napkins for the table and they don't match the candles; or that your sister-in-law constantly snipes because your younger brother has – yet again – made alternative plans to holiday abroad. If mum and dad like their family around them at Christmas, grin and bear it! Remember the pagan concept of sacrifice... but avoid the urge to roast your four-year-old niece instead of the turkey.

That said, if mum and dad are no longer around, there is no earthly reason you should be expected to endure the unendurable that families insist on inflicting on each other at this time of year. Make it known – well in advance – you will be 'home alone' for Yule and intend enjoying it. Having come from a family where Christmas revolved around my father and grandfather, it was difficult to maintain the enthusiasm following their deaths, but the thought of spending 'the Day' solitary never entered the equation. It was my good friend Polly, who changed my way of thinking because she'd spent 'the Day' alone for years and actually looked forward to it. Her preparations were no less enthusiastic with all her favourite foods and a couple of bottles of her chosen tipple shopped for well in advance. From Christmas Eve the candles and fire were lit, with a boxed set ready for the watching, and a selfie-present of a good book, she and the dog snuggled in for two days of sheer indulgence without any interference (or criticism) from outside. When my turn came for the solitary Yule, I made my preparations in advance and enjoyed it, too!

I must confess that I always treat myself to a *very* expensive present, but unfortunately, gift-buying has escalated out of all proportion and this is the main objection a large number of pagans (and non-pagans) have against this annual consumer-fest. Of course the season itself has also changed out of all recognition since those ancient times what with precession, calendar reforms, cultural changes and global warming. So, for the purpose of our own pagan Yuletide festivities, the celebration will begin on the first day of the Roman Saturnalia and end on Old Twelfth Night, according to the Julian calendar, as our medieval ancestors would have observed it. And if you're spending the big day solitary, you need to make sure that everything you do and eat has been especially selected to cater for *your* tastes – and yours alone.

Although greenery has always played a big part in Mid-Winter decorations, it was Prince Albert, husband of Queen Victoria, who popularised the Christmas tree in Britain. In 1841 he brought one over from Germany and set it up in Windsor Castle and real Christmas trees have remained popular ever since. In the past, were not to be brought in, let alone decorated, until after noon on Christmas Eve. The British Christmas Tree Growers Association (BCTGA), however, says it's fine to get them from December 1st onwards, but suggests the middle of the festive season; after Advent (December 11th) is a good compromise, otherwise they've dropped every needle by Boxing Day. Aficionados of the artificial tree often deck the trees anywhere from mid-November onwards.

Here's a complete festive calendar with some simple rites to affirm your pagan commitment to the Mid-Winter Festival but don't feel obliged to party from Saturnalia until Old Twelfth Night or you might be heading for severe medical and weight problems in the not too distant future.

17th December: 'On the first day of Yuletide...'

17th December and the first day of the Roman **Saturnalia** is as good a benchmark as any for putting up the decorations. Remember they have to last until Old Twelfth Night on the 17th January so bear in mind that a cut tree will be looking a bit tired by then. Choose your decorations to suit yourself, but make sure there's a good supply of candles since this is a celebration of the return of the sun; large bowls of twigs and greenery can be just as effective as a tradition tree with its statutory lights and baubles. Yew boughs – which the Christians believed to be unlucky – are also an attractive alternative. We know the Romans went mad with their entertainments, but here we take a leaf out of the Emperor Augustus's book and go for frugality – and remember that it's the last-minute panic-buying that runs away with the money. So make up your lists (see Chapter Three) and start planning; safely power up the candles once the decorations are in place, and prepare a small Saturnalian supper to toast in the festive season with a hot Irish whiskey.

If there is an open fire then arrange well in advance to burn the Yule log at the Solstice; it won't be one of those monsters that burned for the whole of the Yuletide festivities in the past, but even a token log will suffice. Traditionally it should be seasoned oak, ash or fruit-tree wood and be large enough to burn for at least twelve hours and then deliberately extinguished. Originally a Norse tradition, the Yule log is the domestic version of the great community fires of the Mid-Winter Festival and there were time-honoured rituals surrounding its bringing home and kindling. Everyone's attention will be on the coming festivities, just as they have been for thousands of years – as people waited for the longest night to herald the approaching spring.

On the Spiritual Front

Pagans will have made their own provisions for the coming mid-winter celebration to welcome back the Sun-King and among these can be an alternative ash-faggot, made up of ash twigs, to be burned to ensure good fortune. A miniature faggot can be kept in the house for good luck. Like a lot of magical customs, the Yule log must *not* be bought. The hearth fire is the symbolic and magical centre of any pagan home, and it is to the hearth we bring the richness of nature's bounty to help celebrate the old festivals and feast days. Next to the Harvest Home, perhaps the Mid-Winter Festival *is* the most important festival in the pagan calendar so start scavenging for your Yule log – even if it's only a mini ash-faggot for the patio burner! And make sure it is seasoned dry wood to prevent smoking. The Yule log should sit in the hearth until the Winter Solstice, decorated with sprigs of holly.

18th December

Yuletide celebrations are all about feasting and what better time to work out your menus for the Bank Holiday period when all the shops will be closed. If you will be joining friends or family for the traditional Christmas dinner make sure you cater solely for yourself for the remaining meals. Anything that can go in the freezer needs to be bought now (in case shops run out of stock) because then it won't be wasted. There's been a definite downsizing on the supermarket shelves in recent years and by shopping early you'll get the choice of your favourite treats instead of having to make do with what's left. Unless you are a seasoned solitary drinker, resist the urge to stock up on booze for the duration and treat yourself to those individual bottles of prosecco to enjoy rather than guzzle! And what about those tubes of kid's sweets – Smarties, Munchies, Rolos, jelly babies, etc. – which are much cheaper (and a lot more fun) than something disgustingly expensive. If you revert to childhood behind closed doors, who's going to know?

On the Spiritual Front
Make a small advance offering of Mid-Winter fare to the guardians of your hearth and indulge in a quiet moment of contemplation.

19th December: Sigillaria
This was a day of gift-giving in ancient Rome and should be the day set aside for any last gift-buying excursions in order to avoid the crowds frantically doing *their* last-minute shopping in five days' time. It might also be a good time to deliver any long-distance presents so you're not leaving things to the last minute and rushing around like a scalded cat when you should be enjoying the moment. The custom of gift-giving stretches right through the Mid-Winter Festival, so start exploring the local pound shops to see what bargains you can find before the Christmas rush – in fact, start this preparation earlier in the year and you'll be laughing.

On the Spiritual Front
As part of the spirit of giving, buy extra bird food for the visitors to your garden.

20th December
The pagan pantry should be stocked with all kinds of pickles and preserves made during the autumn, including delicious home-made mince-meat. This is the day or evening for entertaining

family and friends and creating a homely atmosphere of warmth and hospitality to compensate others for the fact that you're opting out of their Christmas festivities. Visitors should be offered mulled wine and a mince pie since it is said that by eating a 'mincie' at twelve different houses would guarantee good fortune in the twelve months that follow.

On the Spiritual Front

Privately make a libation of port or red wine to attract warmth and merriment to your home for the whole of the Mid-Winter Festival.

21ˢᵗ December: Winter Solstice

Astronomically speaking, winter begins at the **Winter Solstice**, which falls on or around the 21ˢᵗ and marks the coldest and darkest time of the year when nature sleeps. It is the time of the Holly King who rules the land until the Spring Equinox that occurs in March. If there isn't a holly tree in the garden keep a few sprigs indoors to honour the Dark Lord and his Wild Hunt. Professor E O James in *Seasonal Feasts and Festivals* confirms that:

> Around the Christmas Festival, a great variety of ancient seasonal customs and beliefs from a number of different sources clustered, originally observed from the beginning of November [old Hallowe'en] to the end of January [Candlemas], particularly those connected with the winter solstice rites...

One of those sources was the birthday of Mithras, hailed as an angel and guardian of the sun's light and principal deity of the Roman Legions. This is still an Iranian festival celebrating the passing of the Winter Solstice and now widely known as **Yalda**; an alternative name is Zayesh-e Meher meaning 'Birth of Mithra'. At the turning point of the Winter Solstice, as the longest night of the year and the beginning of the lengthening of days, *Shabe Yaldā* is an

Iranian festival celebrating the victory of light and goodness over darkness and evil. *Shabe Yaldā* means 'birthday eve'.

On the Spiritual Front

For those of pagan belief, the Winter Solstice should be celebrated with all the gusto with which non-pagans approach Christmas Day in terms of feasting. If it should be necessary to attend a family Christmas dinner on the 25th, then a formal supper provides an authentic alternative that can be shared with pagan friends (see Chapter Four). Back in the day, when we had family obligations, the Winter Solstice was welcomed in with a formal dinner where the guests were required to wear black tie and evening dress in order to make the night extra special. By comparison, Christmas dinner a few days later was very informal, indeed! So, put your own stamp on the Night and welcome in the changing of the tide in time-honoured fashion.

22nd **December: Yalda**

According to Persian mythology, Mithra was born at dawn to a virgin mother. He symbolises light, truth, goodness, strength, and friendship; Herodotus reported that this was the most important holiday of the year for contemporary Persians. In more modern times, Persians (Iran) celebrated **Yalda** by staying up late or all night, a practice known as *Shab Chera* meaning 'night gazing'. Fruits and nuts were eaten, especially pomegranates and watermelons, whose red colour invokes the crimson hues of dawn and symbolises the birth of the god. If the skies are clear we might also observe the custom of star-gazing and look for a shooting star from the Ursids meteor shower to make a wish.

On the Spiritual Front

A good opportunity to hold a vigil or watch from late evening of the 21st to dawn on the 22nd to attracted any 'received wisdom' from Otherworld. Collect the ash from the Yule log in a jar and keep it to sprinkle on your Mid-Winter fire next year.

23rd December: Laurentalia

End of Saturnalia and the festival of **Laurentalia** for Acca Larentia, an early Italian goddess of the Earth to whom the seed was entrusted. This is a good time to buy a few packets of wild flower seeds to sow in the spring in her honour. If you're a keen gardener, begin making your selection from the commercial seed catalogues and get a head start on the neighbours.

On the Spiritual Front

This is the time of short days and long, dark nights although we can be sure to witness some spectacular sunrises and sunsets as the rays tinge the frosty landscape a delicate pink. The low sun casts squat shadows along the hedgerow, while deep in the woods there is a frozen stillness, except for the rooks circling noisily overhead. In the stillness of the frozen morning, high overhead a robin thrills out its melodious song. Scatter seed for the birds in a spirit of giving and make time for observing the beauty of the natural world.

24th December: Modraniht

The Anglo-Saxon **Modraniht** or Mother's Night and the beginning of the 'Time Between the Years' – the thirteen sacred days and twelve sacred nights of a Germanic sacrificial festival associated with the 'Matron cult' of the West Germanic peoples on the one hand, and to the *disablót* already known from medieval Scandinavia. This was the blót (sacrificial holiday) held in honour of the female spirits or deities from pre-historic times until the Christianisation of Scandinavia. It is another opportunity to hold an informal party for close non-pagan friends on what they would see as Christmas Eve.

On the Spiritual Front

A sacred date in the calendar and a perfect time for honouring the maternal members of the family with a special gift; and a special time for those of the Heathen Tradition to honour their female deities. We are given a clue as to how the early Anglo Saxons celebrated Yuletide thanks to the 8th century scholar, Bede, who tells us:

> They began the year with December 25, the day we now celebrate as Christmas; and the very night to which we attach special sanctity [Christmas Eve] they designated by the heathen mothers' night – a name bestowed, I suspect, on account of the ceremonies they performed while watching this night through.

Its purpose was to enhance the coming harvest, so scatter bread and wine on the ground in homage.

25th December: *Dies Natalis Solis Invicti*

The renewal of light and the coming of the New Year was celebrated in the later Roman Empire at the **Dies Natalis Solis Invicti**, the 'birthday of the Unconquerable Sun'. This day is the usual bone of contention when resentful pagans throw up their hands and shout: 'I hate Christmas!' – especially when well-meaning friends and neighbours insist on sharing a traditional meal because: 'You don't want to be on your own on Christmas Day!' The answer is, of course, *'Yes, I do!'* and risk giving offense. If you're not eating out, this is a day to batten down the hatches with all the things you like to eat, snuggle up warm with the dog (or cat), a boxed set on the telly – and enjoy. Warn everyone well beforehand that this is your intention and you *don't* want to be disturbed.

On the Spiritual Front

Observe the night by (safely) lighting up the house with dozens of candles to welcome back the sun...and feast well if not wisely on this occasion.

26th December: Boxing Day or St Stephen's Day

The Feast of Stephen (of the Christmas carol fame) fell on this day and so he came to play a part in the Yuletide celebrations, which were previously associated with Freyr. The Romans are believed to have brought the idea of collecting boxes to Britain, and monks and clergy soon implemented similar boxes to collect money for the poor at Christmas. On the day after Christmas, the priests used to open the boxes and distribute the contents to the needy of the village. The modern version originated in England in the middle of the 19th century under Queen Victoria. When servants prepared to leave to visit their families, their employers would present them with gift boxes; it was also the custom on that day for tradesmen to collect their Christmas boxes or gifts in return for good and reliable service throughout the year. As it was the servants' day off, employers and their families would traditionally be forced to have cold meats for the main meal of the day.

On the Spiritual Front

Make a generous donation to the charity of your choice.

27th December: Mari Lwyd

The **Mari Lwyd** is a wassailing folk custom found in South Wales and under other names in various parts of England. The tradition entails the use of an eponymous hobby horse, which is made from a horse's skull mounted on a pole and carried by an individual hidden under a sackcloth. It represents a regional variation of a 'hooded animal' tradition that appears in various forms throughout Britain. Folklorist E C Cawte thought it more likely that the term had originally meant 'Grey Mare', thus referring to the heads' equine appearance, which is highly significant within traditional British Old Craft. The Mari Lwyd custom was performed during the winter festivities, specifically around the dates of Christmas and New Year. However, the precise date on which the custom was performed varied between villages, and in a number of cases the custom was carried out for several consecutive nights. Make sure there's plenty of music in your home.

On the Spiritual Front

Pour a libation of port or red wine and offer it to the spirit of the ancestors – whatever your tradition.

28th December

Many of the traditions and customs associated with Christmas and the New Year (see example above) are taken from the numerous Victorian compilations that stripped away all the ancient practices and re-labelled the superstitions as 'unlucky'. There is a tremendous amount of pagan folklore hidden away in these texts that often speak aloud to those well-versed in the Old Ways. So don't dismiss folklore and superstitions as 'nonsense' since there might be more wisdom contained in the customs than you realise.

On the Spiritual Front

Make a resolution to learn more about the history of your chosen path or tradition and join the Folklore Society if you are not already a member.

29th December

With everything quietening down for a few days before the 'new' New Year celebrations begin, it might be a good time to offer thanks to the 'powers that be' for all the good things that have happened during the past year.

On the Spiritual Front

Those of a traditional Craft persuasion will be out and about at dawn and dusk to utilise the magical energies of this 'time between times', especially at the boundaries and borders of the field margin. It may not be conducive for elaborate outdoor ritual, but there is still a great deal of magical energy to be drawn from the landscape to help recharge the batteries by just taking the dog for a walk.

30ᵗʰ December

Fortune-telling was always a popular pastime at Christmas family gatherings, with grandmothers amusing the children by reading the tea-leaves or playing cards.

On the Spiritual Front

As the year draws to its close we can take a peek into the future by the various divination methods to see what precautions we can take to ward off ill-luck. Divination by flames to foretell the future is thought to be one of the first methods ever used. The intensity of the flames, as well as the shape and form they take, is considered when divining the future or interpreting omens. The 'Witch's Yuletide Divination' taken from *Traditional Witchcraft for Fields & Hedgerows* suggests:

> If a sprig of holly is thrown on the fire and burns with a crackling noise, it is a sign that the auspices will be fine; but if it burns with a dull flame and does not crackle, it is a sign that all will not be well in the coming year.

31ˢᵗ December: 'New' New Year's Eve or Hogmanay

Hogmanay is the Scots word for the last day of the year and synonymous with the celebration of the New Year (in the Gregorian calendar) in the Scottish manner. The origins of Hogmanay are unclear, but may derive from Norse and Gaelic observances. Customs vary throughout Scotland, and usually include gift-giving and visiting the homes of friends and neighbours with special attention given to the custom of first-footing – honouring the first guest of the New Year. For the rest of us there are numerous parties out there, even if it's only a regular date with Jools Holland on television.

On the Spiritual Front

Any dark-haired man in the family should be sent outside and only re-enter the house on the last stroke of midnight, preferably bringing a piece of coal for the fire. It's a kind gesture to extend the 'first footing' to neighbours' homes, too.

1st January: Feast Day of Strenia

Strenia is the old Sabine goddess of good health, and in her name gifts were exchanged for good luck. Hogmanay is normally followed by further celebration on the morning of New Year's Day (1st January) or, in some cases, 2nd January – a Scottish bank holiday. Small tokens of friendship can be given, but even as late as the early 1900s the old Roman custom of *strena* was still being observed in rural parts of South Wales. Small boys would collect the *calenning* (New Year gifts of pennies and small cakes) although the practice of decorating oranges and apples had largely died out. The fruit was pierced with corn, holly and mistletoe and stuck with three skewers to serve as a stand when not being held. A fourth skewer acted as a handle.

On the Spiritual Front

The *strena* was a Roman symbol of fruitfulness for the coming year. Make your own and let it stand by the front door to attract 'wealth' during the coming months. Dispose of it by leaving the stripped apple outside for the birds.

2nd January

The traditional day when most people go back to work... and an ideal time for making those New Year's resolutions. Forget the usual broken promises to diet, give up smoking/drinking, or anything else that takes your fancy on the spur of the moment – try to come up with something really useful and sustainable.

On the Spiritual Front

Make a resolution that you will pay more attention to the old rites and customs relating to your pagan beliefs. The more firmly entrenched you are in the customs of your belief, the easier life becomes.

3rd January: Perihelion

The point during the year when the Earth is closest to the sun occurs around this date. Currently, the Earth reaches perihelion in early January, approximately 14 days after the Winter Solstice. At perihelion, the Earth's centre is about 91,402,500 miles from the sun's centre.

On the Spiritual Front

Light a special beeswax or gold coloured candle in honour of the sun and let it burn out.

4th January: Wrenning

Although the wren has always enjoyed a certain protection as a sacred bird, on one day of the year it was hunted and killed – **Wrenning**. As an example of transference magic, the wren was expected to shoulder all the ills and problems of the people; effectively taking their bad luck, ill health, and so forth, leaving them free to hope for good health and prosperity in the coming year. Traditionally, the tree of the wren is the ivy, while the robin is allocated the holly.

On the Spiritual Front

A simple rite from *Traditional Witchcraft for Fields & Hedgerows* that could be performed instead of the actual killing of a wren could be as follows:

A traditional substitute for a wren was a ball of sheep wool collected from the hedgerow and dyed brown. In the late afternoon before the Winter Solstice, visit your local hedgerow and ritually cut a length of *flowering* ivy, stating as you do so, that you are honouring the spirit of the Old Year. Wrap the ivy in a piece of silk and carry it home. Place the ivy in a central part of the house, where it can absorb all the dross accrued over the year – perhaps as part of the festive decorations. At dawn of Twelfth Night, re-wrap the ivy in its silk and, together with the wool, return to the hedge. Locate a strong *male* holly tree and wind the ivy and wool round the base of the trunk, stating your intention. Offer thanks to the spirit of the ivy/wren and then leave the ivy to die.

The intention of this ritual is to offer the life force of the old year in sacrifice to the spirit of the new, so that it can flourish with extra vigour (as will your own fortune). Light a small fire and burn the silk (silk headscarves can be obtained quite cheaply from most charity shops). This represents the destroying aspect of the goddess and by performing this rite, you will have enacted the entire birth-death-regenerative cycle. The reason why the traditional Midwinter 'hunting of the wren' now takes place in early January is because the shift from the Julian to the Gregorian calendar meant eleven days were lost in the process.

(Note that male holly trees do not have berries, while the females are the berry-bearing trees.)

5th January: Twelfth Night

Currently the last day of the Christmas season and the night for wassailing and **Twelfth Night** celebrations. Traditionally, the wassail is celebrated on Twelfth Night while some still wassail on 'Old Twelvey Night' – 17th January – as it would have been before the introduction of the Gregorian calendar. In the cider-producing West of England (primarily the counties of Devon, Somerset,

Dorset, Gloucestershire and Herefordshire) wassailing also refers to drinking (and singing) the health of trees in the hopes that they might better thrive. The purpose of wassailing is to awake the cider apple trees and to scare away evil spirits to ensure a good harvest of fruit in the coming autumn. Then the assembled crowd would sing and shout and bang drums or pots and pans and generally make a terrible racket until the guns-men gave a great final volley through the branches to make sure the work was done and then off they went to the next orchard. Chinese crackers, or even party poppers, will suffice if you haven't got a gun licence. A belief has arisen in modern times in some English-speaking countries that it is unlucky to leave Christmas decorations hanging after Twelfth Night, a tradition originally attached to the festival of Candlemas (2nd February) that marked the end of the long ecclesiastical season that ran from Advent to Candlemas Eve.

On the Spiritual Front
Raise a glass of cider or apple juice in honour of the old custom if celebrating Twelfth Night tonight, and if there are fruit trees in the garden pour a libation.

6th January: Old Christmas Day
This is according to the Julian calendar, which is still celebrated in Ireland as *Nollaig na mBan*, 'Little Christmas' or 'Women's Christmas'. It goes back to the days when large families were the norm and men never lifted a finger in the house to help, and were never expected to. But each year, after the Christmas holiday, tired women finally got a break – for one day, at least. On 6th January, men would take over the housework, giving their womenfolk a chance to go out to relax with each other. It is still regarded by many as the end of the Christmas season.

On the Spiritual Front
Treat the lady of the house to a special day out and make it

something really memorable.

Plough Monday

This is the traditional start of the English agricultural year and while local customs may vary, Plough Monday is generally the first Monday after Twelfth Day on 6th January. References to Plough Monday date back to the late 15th century, which means the festivities would have coincided with the old Julian calendar. The traditional Norfolk 'Plough Pudding' is a boiled suet pudding, containing meat and onions and eaten on Plough Monday.

7th January: St Distaff's Day

This was traditionally when women resumed their household work after the holiday.

On the Spiritual Front

Make an additional resolution to help more with the daily household chores.

8th January

On 8th January 1851, using a device known as **Foucault's pendulum**, Frenchman Léon Foucault demonstrated that the Earth rotates on its axis. He discovered that if a long pendulum with a heavy weight was set swinging, the plane in which it was swinging would appear to rotate. The direction in the path showed movement of the Earth against the swing of the pendulum.

On the Spiritual Front

Perhaps this is a good day to consult the pendulum for advice on how to approach the coming year. For any pagan a pendulum should be a constant companion and consulted over any major changes taking place. Keep it in a special pouch so no one else can handle it.

9th January

With the Mid-Winter festivities winding down, today might provide an opportunity to develop the art of 'standing and staring' in order to reconnect with the natural world.

On the Spiritual Front

Take time to go for a long walk and observe the beauty of nature's blank canvas.

10th January

The importance of 'beginnings' is one of the fundamental principles of superstition in the British Isles. The New Year is an obvious addition to this list, and for those (usually non-pagan) who are prone to superstition almost anything that happens at New Year can be taken as ominous; activities which, if they occurred at any other time of the year, would be regarded as simple happenings, often take on the role of potentially luck-enhancing signs.

On the Spiritual Front

Spend a few moments to acknowledge all the gods of the old world and pour a libation for luck in the coming year. If we behave in a manner that confirms our belief in the Old Ones, then they will continue to believe in us.

11th January: Juturna, Carmentalia and Old New Year's Eve

Juturna is the Roman goddess of fountains and the underworld whose symbol is a spring; this was an ancient fire festival still celebrated as Old New Year even after the calendar reforms. It is also **Carmentalia**, the feast day of the Roman goddess of prophecy. **Old New Year's Eve**, according to the Julian calendar, is a time to see in the New Year with friends of pagan persuasion who might have been tied up with family obligations over the earlier holiday.

On the Spiritual Front

Let each guest pour a libation of port or wine and make a wish as the clock chimes midnight. This might be an opportune moment to cast the Tarot cards and see what the future has in store for you over the next few months between now and the Spring Equinox, or consult your own favourite method of divining.

12ᵗʰ January: Handsel

Among the rural population of Scotland, *Auld Hansel Monday* is traditionally celebrated on the first Monday after January 12ᵗʰ, reflecting a reluctance to switch from the old style calendar to the new one. The word originates from Old Saxon meaning 'to deliver into the hand' and refers to small tips and gifts of money given as a token of good luck, particularly at the beginning of something; the modern house-warming gift would be a good example. In this respect it is somewhat similar to Boxing Day, which eventually supplanted it. The firm conviction that the special character of **Old New Year's Day** was reflected in the natural world held that whoever succeeded in drawing the first water – known as the *creame* – from any well (spring) would be lucky.

On the Spiritual Front

Go to a local well or spring and drink from it, or sprinkle a few drops over your head, to affirm your allegiance to the Old Ways. Well dressing and holy wells are another pagan observation absorbed by the Church because the sanctity of sacred wells and springs dates back to extremely ancient times.

13ᵗʰ January: St Hilary's Day

This feast day has gained the reputation of being the coldest day of the year due to past cold events starting on or around this date. One of the most severe winters in history began around 13ᵗʰ January in 1205, when the Thames froze over; ale and wine turned to solid ice and were sold by weight. In 1086, a great frost also started spreading over the country on St Hilary's Day; and after whom the 'Hilary term' in some universities and law courts is named.

On the Spiritual Front

Light a candle at the hearth on the morning to symbolise the keeping of cold at bay, and let it burn out without extinguishing it.

14th January

Despite the earlier alterations, by the 21st century the Julian calendar is now thirteen days behind the Gregorian calendar, thus January 14th is sometimes celebrated as New Year's Day (Old New Year) by the many religious groups who still use the old calendar.

On the Spiritual Front

Burn a candle and offer a libation of wine honouring your affiliation to the Old Ways.

15th January

As we approach the end of the festive season it is a good time to reflect on the direction our own belief/faith will lead us in the coming year.

On the Spiritual Front

Make a small donation or take any unwanted gifts to a local charity.

16th January: National Religious Freedom Day

This commemorates the adoption of Thomas Jefferson's landmark Virginia Statute for Religious Freedom on January 16, 1786, that led to freedom of religion for all Americans, officially proclaimed on January 16th each year by an annual statement by the President of the United States. By contrast, **Nothing Day** is an 'un-event' also observed annually on January 16th since 1973, when it was added to *Chase's Calendar of Events*. It is not actually a public holiday in the US, as that requires an act of Congress, and its purpose is to provide Americans with one national day when they can just sit without celebrating, observing or honouring anything!

On the Spiritual Front
Light a candle for all pagans who have died or suffered for their beliefs.

17ᵗʰ January: Old Twelfth Night
In some places **Old Twelfth Night** is still celebrated on this evening, continuing the custom on the date determined by the Julian calendar. It is an ideal time to observe the close of the pagan Yuletide season with a party – possibly with a fancy dress party – that echoes the revelry and merriment of Tudor times. There was also a darker side to Twelfth Night and it seems to have been widely believed that during this mid-winter period, spirits of many kinds stirred abroad, and not all of them beneficent. The dead also returned and in some regions it was considered safer to stay indoors at night – these were probably the spirits of the dead who had returned at Hallowe'en and were having a last fling before returning to Otherworld! This is also the feast day of **Felicitas**, the Roman personification of good fortune, happiness or felicity.

On the Spiritual Front
If not partying, drink a toast to the Old Ways and the ancestors on this old Twelfth Night and observe it by watching one of the many DVD versions of the Shakespeare play.

Calendars
The modern calendar often throws up a few anomalies that can be confusing to pagans unfamiliar with the history and customs of their tradition. By rule of thumb, the celebrations for Saturnalia and Yule are governed by the Winter Solstice, which is astronomically fixed to fall on or around the 21ˢᵗ December. Christmas Day, however, is a calendar date that was altered by the eleven 'lost'

days when the old Julian calendar was exchanged for the Gregorian one. Hence some people still celebrate 'old Christmas', 'old New Year' and 'old Twelfth Night'. Contemporary pagans may find it easier to adhere to the modern calendar, but traditionalists will continue to work by the old calendar – not just at the Mid-Winter Festival, but for the rest of the year, too.

Chapter Three

Let the Revels Begin

The Circle ritual for December conducted at the Winter Solstice should acknowledge that from this yearly death a new countryside will emerge, 'vital and lush with springtime's fertile breath'. The Yule log symbolises the idea of this rebirth of light, i.e. the sun. The Mid-Winter Festival is the start of longer, lighter days as the Lord of the Sun arises from the Lady of the Land.

In order to run smoothly, our pagan Mid-Winter Festival/Yule needs to be planned well in advance and not be spoiled by any last-minute disasters. A bit of organisation goes a long way so start by making lists to cover all aspects of the festivities – guests, gifts and gormandising. As far as the guests go, our choices will probably fall into three categories:

- A traditional Christmas Day with family
- A traditional Yule with pagan friends
- A solitary pagan Mid-Winter celebration

With regard to the first option, in the preface to the original 1938 version of *Larousse Gastronomique*, Auguste Escoffier wrote: 'The history of the table of a nation is a reflection of the civilisation of that nation…' and for 'Christmas: Noël', the entry read:

In France, the main Christmas meal is served on the night of 24th to 25th December [Christmas Eve] after the celebration of Midnight Mass. This meal is called the *réveillon*. The menu of the *réveillon* and of Christmas Day itself – essentially a family celebration – must include dishes which have, so to speak, a ritual significance. However rich the dishes in the *réveillon* menu, even if they include expensive delicacies such as foie gras, truffles, game of various kinds, rare fish and shellfish, they must also include, in deference to tradition, a black or white pudding, sometimes both, and a goose or turkey with chestnuts, which, naturally, are often enriched with truffles.

In Britain Christmas Day is celebrated gastronomically with even more splendour than in France. 'For many of the islanders,' wrote Alfred Suzanne in his book *La Cuisine anglaise et américaine* (English and American cookery) 'this anniversary is memorable (apart from all religious significance) because it evokes a great slaughter of turkeys, geese and all kinds of game, a wholesale massacre of fat oxen, pigs and sheep; they envisage garlands of black puddings, sausages and saveloys... mountains of plum-puddings and oven-fulls of mince pies... On that day no one in England may go hungry... This is a family gathering, and on every table the same menu is prepared. A joint of beef, a turkey or goose, which usually the *pièce de rèsistance*, accompanied by a ham, sausages and game; then follow the inevitable plum pudding and the famous mince pies'.

If we tried to eat like that today, the entire family would be comatose until New Year, or suffer a coronary by Candlemas – and just imagine how much waste there would have been since refrigeration was in its infancy. Nevertheless, it does reflect the kind of Christmas catering our parents or grandparents would have considered normal during the years leading up to WWII. Most families are more frugal these days, but it's still the excess that most pagans, and an increasing number of non-pagans, find off-putting about a traditional family Christmas.

But it's not all cheer and goodwill on the non-pagan front. Apparently one of the biggest stresses people feel is financial and in a recent study in the United States, 45 per cent of people said they'd prefer to skip Christmas altogether because of the financial strain it puts on them. And when you think that Irish shoppers spend more than their European counterparts, with an average minimum spend of over €600 per person on presents, clothes, booze and food, there has to be a better way of maxing the credit card than paying out on what is no more than just a single gargantuan roast dinner! There are ways of celebrating Yuletide on a tight budget and all it takes is a little bit of advanced planning. Hence the necessity of list-making mentioned earlier.

Traditional Family Christmas

The customary family pattern begins to emerge in October with the casual question: 'Have you thought what you're doing about Christmas?'

If you come from a family that operates a strict rota system this can simplify things, but as the years creep by there are subtle changes to the dynamics of the family group. Different in-laws, marital differences, divorces, new partners, logistical problems, not to mention off-spring of varying ages. These all contribute to the loaded question about who's doing what for Christmas. Everyone is hoping that someone else will issue the invite, offer to travel, take the difficult relative – or even make the alternative suggestion that Christmas lunch at a local hotel might offer the perfect solution. Or everyone might be waiting to see who backs down first and offer to host the festivities.

If there's no escape from spending 'the Day' with mum and dad, then work out the calendar well in advance in order to keep the number of days down to a minimum. Perhaps *you* suggest doing something different – like going to a hotel for the Christmas break, lunch at a local restaurant, or even a mini cruise! Old habits are very difficult to break, so try not to cause upset by forcing the issue; and if you can persuade them around to your way of thinking, make sure you make the reservations early because the best places are fully booked by the beginning of October.

On a more modest level, and especially if there are several siblings involved, set down your own rules early in the year about the cost of presents and a share of the workload, i.e. the maximum £/$/€ per person you are willing to spend, and confirm you will be providing the starter and/or dessert for Christmas dinner. No need to feel awful if your family exceeds that amount on a gift, or doesn't want to eat your contribution; leave a little bit of room for negotiation, but try to stick to your guns.

If, on the other hand, mum and dad are no longer alive then there is no earthly reason why you should be subjecting yourself to two days of misery with other relatives or in-laws who you never otherwise see and perhaps can't stand either. Even loved siblings can have dreaded in-laws who make the enjoyment of any event an impossibility. Once you've made up your mind that *you* have no intention of participating in another traditional family Christmas then the battle-lines need to be drawn early. So around the Autumn Equinox state quite categorically that you will be making alternative plans for the Mid-Winter Festival – and if necessary lie a little about what you will be doing at this stage. Just make the point early enough so the family gets used to the idea.

A Traditional Yule with Pagan Friends

Perhaps you're opting for a traditional Yule with some pagan friends that will avoid all the elements you object to about Christmas. The festival still needs to be planned with some degree of precision if it's going to be a success. Pagan children love toys and gifts just as much as their non-pagan counterparts – so not much change there, then – but keep the gifts within budget. You may also decide that a tree – real or artificial – is *passé* or just ecological unsound, but there's plenty of room for large displays of greenery and twigs.

Work out who is being invited to each of the important celebration: Winter Solstice, *Sol Invictus*, New Year, Twelfth Night or anything else in between. Are you going to theirs, or are they coming to you? Some of your friends might have family obligations of their own and not be available for the important festivals, so compile your guest list accordingly. A simple supper with like-minded people can be just as much fun as filling the house with semi-strangers and loading up a groaning dining room table – and there's less clearing up afterwards, too.

A Solitary Pagan Mid-Winter Celebration

If, on the other hand, we've decided to spend the Mid-Winter Festival alone, then the same rules still apply. It can be rather daunting to actually plan for a solitary Yule, but since the whole focus of the holiday is usually getting together with those close to you – and if those people are no longer around – then the exercise is pointless.

The solitary life-style is amplified at this time of year and all the hype that is geared around spending time with family often creates the impression that if you're not part of the glamour then you're nothing but a sad git! There's a vast difference, however, between being alone and being lonely. And although outsiders might think it a bit strange, the company of a cat or dog means that there's someone in the home to talk to and snuggle up with, and discuss what we're going to watch on telly.

Planning a Timetable

So let's plan a timetable of which of those 32 days we want to observe and who we want to spend them with. For example, the most important days are:

Putting up the Decorations

These can be a simple or lavish as we choose and if we're going for the 'tree and baubles' style, that's fine; so is having bowls of twigs or greenery decked with that thin metallic tape used for wrapping presents. Available in red, gold and silver, there's yards of the stuff and it can be made to curl by running it between your thumb and a blunt knife. This event can be planned for any day between the start of Saturnalia and the Winter Solstice, and can be good fun if friends are involved. Back in the summer we need to select what will be our Yule log, either in token or as the largest log we can fit into the hearth, or outside in the fire pit/burner. This is because the timber should be well-seasoned (i.e. thoroughly dried out) in order to burn well during our mid-winter celebrations. The log should be decorated with sprigs of holly and sit in the hearth until the Winter Solstice. Mulled wine or hot Irish whiskies are the order of the day, together with finger or fork food that is easy to eat.

Winter Solstice

This is the time for having pagan guests for supper and together you can make this into an important annual celebration. As I've said earlier, I always made this into a very formal evening with all the white linen (laundered in advance), silver and glassware in use for the occasion – together with a traditional menu to match. Keep the group small and intimate since the secret to a good supper party is not the food, but the right mix of people. Much will depend on your guest's individual food requirements. Many pagans are vegetarian – if this is the case, don't be afraid to ask for help because there is nothing less welcoming that offering someone a plate of plain vegetables while others tuck into meat or fish. This is all part of the advance planning – so start your own tradition.

Dies Natalis Solis Invicti, or 'the Day'

This is the day that needs to have plenty of candles around and if you choose to start by opening your presents by candle/fire light with a glass of prosecco, then you'll not go far wrong during the rest of the day unless you've consumed the whole bottle before ten o' clock. In the spirit of gift-giving treat yourself to a book, DVD and CD aimed at making the day and the next pass pleasantly. If you don't fancy cooking, treat yourself to something luxurious and oven-ready from M&S or Lidl's luxury range for your dinner/supper, together with the tipple of your choice. Light the fire, tuck up under your favourite throw and chill.

New Year's Eve

Most people celebrate New Year's Eve with friends on 31st December, but if you want to observe the old New Year as the ancestors would have done, hold your own pagan event on 11th January (or the 14th). Nothing to stop you having a typical New Year's bash, but this one is eleven (or thirteen) days later according to custom and it won't interfere with other people's party plans.

Twelfth Night

Similarly, Twelfth Night has also been thrown out of sync and instead of observing it on 5th January, some people wait until the 17th and throw a party to celebrate the end of the Mid-Winter Festival with true medieval gusto. Ideally, a fancy dress party would seem to be the order of the day, but how long your mid-winter revels last will, of course, depend on how much time you have off work during the party season and your personal stamina!

Get Outside

Regardless of how you decide to spend Yuletide, don't stay cooped up at home the whole time... get out for a walk. A long walk in a new location can do wonders to lighten the mood and blow away the cobwebs. As I mentioned in *Traditional Witchcraft for Urban Living*, and although many pagans would probably have conniptions at the suggestion, one of the most effective places for peace and meditation for the urban witch is often a local church, especially if its foundations are very old. Remember that early churches were built on existing pagan sites where the hallowed pagan aura is probably less polluted than at the majestic crowd-pullers of Avebury and Stonehenge! Be conscious of the tranquillity and history of the building and not the division between beliefs. Go on, try it!

In the days between the Winter Solstice and 'the Day' take time to wander through your town or village – with all the shopping done it's a time to stand and stare – and dare I say, enjoy the community feel to the place. And treat yourself to a relaxed pub lunch or afternoon tea while drinking in the atmosphere of Yule without the necessity of becoming embroiled in all the brouhaha of last-minute panic buying. We have the satisfaction of knowing all our victuals are bought, the presents dispersed and all that's left for us to do is enjoy the magic of the season – ours not theirs!

Time Between the Years

Actually, it's a lot of fuss for just two days and the time between St Stephen's Day and new New Year's Eve is like 'slack water' – a metaphor we can use for this magically confused time of the season. Slack water, which used to be known as 'the stand of the tide', is a short period in a body of tidal water when the water is completely unstressed, and therefore no movement either way in the tidal stream, which occurs before the direction of the tidal stream reverses. It is a continuance of the Anglo-Saxon idea of 'Time Between the Years' – those thirteen sacred days and twelve sacred nights that began at Modraniht – a pause between the past and the future when our personal divinational skills can be brought into play.

Divination is the prediction of future events, or the 'discovery of secret matters by a great variety of means, signs and occult techniques'. Since the beginning of civilisation, people have always wanted to see into the future and it's been said that divination was as commonplace in the past as satellite communication is today: it was part of everyday life. Nevertheless, whatever method is used to predict the future, those results are not cast in stone! Divination reveals the future as relating to the past and the present, and what will happen if the warnings are not heeded in order to change things *before* they go wrong. At this 'Time Between The Years' it is a perfect opportunity for attempting to divine what the coming year has in store for us… and what we can do to circumnavigate any potential difficulties.

New Year's Eve to Twelfth Night

From New Year's Eve to Twelfth Night the tide begins to turn and the Earth's natural cycle begins to move again. The days grow longer and the Earth-tides grow stronger. Whether we observe the Julian or the Gregorian calendar there is an upbeat feeling to the start of the New Year. Make sure that a thorough banishing and cleansing of your home has been carried out on the day following Twelfth Night to remove any negative psychic energies that might be lurking about.

The Circle ritual for January should reflect the celebration of new beginnings. Collect firewood or kindling as a symbolic gesture and make a supply of miniature faggots (bundles) for burning during magical workings. Ideally, these should be made from any of the nine sacred woods, ash, birch, yew, hazel, rowan, willow, pine, thorn, or other indigenous trees recognised as being traditionally sacred, with the exception of oak or elder.

Footnote

The taking down of the decorations and disposing of them also has a fair share of superstition surrounding it. The most common belief dating from Victorian times is that all the decorations should be removed on New Year's Day or Twelfth Night/Old Christmas Day; before that time it had been Candlemas at least since the mid 17th century.

According to the old calendar, the festive greenery not taken down by Twelfth Night should be left up until Candlemas Day (2nd February) and then removed. In fact, Candlemas was formerly the date when Christians kept their decorations up as noted in this poem by Robert Herrick (1591-1674), *Ceremony upon Candlemas Eve.*

> Down with the rosemary, and so
> Down with the bays and mistletoe;
> Down with the holly, ivy, all,
> Wherewith ye dress'd the Christmas Hall

Whatever day was chosen for their removal, there was still the vital question of how to dispose of the evergreen. In *The Penguin Guide to the Superstitions of Britain & Ireland*, the author, folklorist Steve Roud, records that a in some areas of Shropshire there was a custom of feeding evergreens used for Christmas decorations to the farm animals. Often the holly was burned, but the ivy was given to the milking cows. Some kept the dried branches to hand and used them to make the fire to cook the pancakes on Shrove Tuesday.

One superstition claimed that if holly was kept in the house after Christmas Day, the 'Evil One' would come and pull *it* down – whether referring to the holly or the house was not specified in local folklore. *Chambers Book of Days* (1864) warned that if every scrap of Christmas decoration was not removed from the church before Candlemas Day, there would be a death within the year in the family occupying the pew where a leaf or berry was left.

There appears to be no discernible regional pattern to explain the different superstitions since in some places it was considered sinful to burn Christmas evergreens, while others claimed it was merely unlucky. It is interesting that, according to Steve Roud, the anti-burning appears to date from c1866, while there are references that mention burning Yuletide decorations right back to the 11th century. This suggests that burning was indeed a pagan custom. At my family home the evergreens were always burned and there was a custom of handing out small 'tree presents' when the tree was stripped. The bonfire of all the evergreens took place on the vegetable patch so that the wood ash could be dug into the soil to promote a good crop in the following months.

Recycling Christmas trees isn't always easy, but there are a few solutions. Many council-run recycling centres shred used Christmas trees to make ground-cover for use in public parks. If you can't get to the tip with your tree, see if your local council provide a collection service. As a pagan, however, you could strip the branches yourself and use the pine needles for *pot pourri* , or cut the tree into small pieces and burn them on an open fire – indoors or out – and enjoy the smell.

Chapter Four

Gifts and Feasting

The most costly (and wasteful) items of a traditional family Christmas are the expensive presents that are now obligatory; and the mountain of food/drink that has to be piled up in the garden shed because there's no room in the fridge/freezer/pantry. For those of you who love statistics – here are a few tips and tricks to help make your festive season a little more eco-friendly.

The Art of Good Gift-Giving

Or as the *Irish Country Living* team would have it on their gift page:

Bright copper kettles and hand-crafted spoons,
Wonderful cake stands for great afternoons.
Beautiful cheese boards tied up in strings
These are a few of our favourite things…

It was rather frightening, however, to discover that 37 per cent of adults said they received gifts worth an average of £54 that they did not want or use; while more than 50 per cent of gifts received were considered to be useless. In a recent survey, when asked which gifts they consider to be the worst or most useless, 60 per cent of women declared suspect-smelling perfume gifts sets as the worst presents they'll receive. Following close behind were bath sets, useless decorative boxes, chick-lit novels, scarves they'd never wear, and the dreaded pair of novelty socks and knickers.

Men were also asked to list the most underwhelming gifts they were likely to receive: dull biographies of personalities in whom they had no interest were damned as the number one most useless present. Next in the useless gift charts were novelty socks and underwear with a huge 46 per cent listing these as their most dreaded gift items. These were followed by 'funny' slogan t-shirts, stress relievers and deodorant sets vying for fourth place. Neither are 'craft' gifts well-received since most of us are pretty abysmal at making things, and *Kirsty's Hand-Made Christmas* stuff certainly gives me the horrors!

The December magazines and colour supplements all feature gift suggestions for him, her and the kids, but 'gifting on a budget' doesn't appear to be in the editors' vocabulary. Yes, a pink Pashmina would be nice (are they still 'in'?), but not one costing £150 – or a horse-racing membership that's going to set you back £300! If you are pleading guilty to 'useless present buying', now's the time to rethink your approach to Yuletide gift giving. Which would you rather receive? A gift that only cost a few pounds that gave you pleasure, or something disgustingly expensive (back to those ultra-posh chocolates, again) that you *really* don't like?

The art of good gift-giving is all in the imagination. Usually we are buying presents for people we know reasonably well and this provides a valuable insight into personal likes and dislikes. Unlike the aunt who was presented with an Argos catalogue by her small niece, who had indicated with the use of a marker-pen all the things she'd like for Christmas! Admittedly not everything cost a fortune, but somehow I felt the true essence of the Christmas spirit was missing with this calculating gesture, especially as this was a devout Catholic family.

Start by budgeting what you realistically want to spend. About £10/£20 per person *is* reasonable providing we intend to put in the time and effort to find just the right gift. One piece of how-two advice on the subject of gift-buying is worth sharing: 'Presents are easy. I begin collecting them in the summer and they are mostly small but carefully chosen at 'X would like that' moments. I don't admit it, but some come from charity shops…' was the view of one weekend columnist.

For instance, I often find that economical gift-buying starts at the garden centre. Not necessarily those expensive pre-planted bowls, but rather a simple pot of hyacinths that will bloom into the New Year and fill any room with a subtle perfume in the dark days of January. These can be obtained from garden centres and supermarkets, and usually cost under a fiver; a tastefully chosen container will add appeal to the gift. Or how about a brightly coloured window-box planter filled with an assortment of herbs for the kitchen? Or a spring-flowering shrub for the garden? And why don't Brits feel comfortable buying plants and flowers for men? These are gifts I would be delighted to receive and nothing costs more than £10.

A small assortment of homemade pickles/preserves in a useful container usually goes down well; as does a selection of quality cheeses that dispenses with the commercial packaging and traditional board. Add grapes, a stick of celery and a packet of good quality crackers and you have a modestly priced gift. Late summer and autumn fairs are the perfect place to shop for these items; or check out the local farmers' market if you're not into making your own. One delightful Yule gift I received many years ago was a large Douwe Egberts coffee jar recycled to hold a wide assortment of the more unusual cooking spices in small, re-sealable clear plastic bags.

In Iceland, which is probably the most officially pagan (Heathen) country in the world, they have a wonderful custom of giving books to each other as gifts on Christmas Eve – and then spending the night reading. This custom is so deeply ingrained in the culture that it is the reason for the *Jolabokaflod*, or 'Christmas Book Flood', when the majority of books in Iceland are sold between September and December in preparation for Christmas giving. People of all ages like books (apart from those ill-chosen biographies) so begin making your Yuletide book-list early in the year. The 'remaindered' bookshops also offer a wide range of titles at bargain prices, especially for children.

Coloured candles are always a welcome gift, but do avoid the scented ones unless the recipient has a known preference. With all the other smells contributing to the Yuletide atmosphere, a cloying perfumed candle can be quite nauseous. The best choice is possibly one of those huge pillar candles that are too expensive to buy for yourself, but are a joy to receive. Decorative outdoor candle contains and lanterns are also welcome presents; as are solar lights.

One idea I rather liked was in a letter entitled, Start a Christmas Tradition:

My girlfriend's family has a great tradition where the grandmother gives everyone a themed Christmas tree ornament from Hallmark, with each person having their own theme (for example, my girlfriend always receives a puppy ornament). Every year everyone looks forward to getting a new Christmas ornament.

There are beautiful tree decorations now available and this was a new 'tradition' I think everyone should adopt!

Wrapping presents is one of the pleasures of Yuletide, but when we consider that the amount of wrapping paper thrown away in the UK alone would stretch to the moon, we might need to think again. One of my greatest successes was using pages from the broadsheet newspapers and tying them with scarlet ribbon; another year it was those *'brown paper packages tied up with string'* and decorated with catkins and cones from an alder tree. An added bonus is that this type of paper is highly recyclable for fire lighting.

Small baskets from previous presents can regularly be found in charity shops throughout the year, so buy whenever you see them and fill them with Yuletide presents using shredded coloured paper as protective packaging around the gifts. In fact, charity shops are one of the best sources for reusable packaging because folk often think some containers are too nice to throw away and off-load them on the charity shop instead. If this isn't your thing, buy different sized Kilner jars for food gifts and decorate them with ribbon.

So, agree your budget with family and friends on the amount to be spent well in advance because people have all sorts of different incomes and it can be a source of embarrassment if there is a noticeable difference in the cost of the gifts exchanged. Plan to have the present side sorted by the beginning of December at the latest and remember: gift-giving doesn't have to be a costly business. The secret is to buy when you see a gift that will delight rather than wait until the present-buying season when the pressure is on.

The Art of Good Feasting

In *Food & Feast in Medieval England*, Peter Hammond reveals that at Christmas 1289, the Bishop of Hereford fed on venison from four deer; a boar's head and braun (made from the meat) were very popular, although by the 16th century domesticated boar had to be used to keep up with the demand.

> Sometimes a Christmas meal was provided for a villain, for example one of the lord's shepherds. In one case it was recorded that a man also received a loaf for his dog on Christmas Day. At Christmas in 1314 in North Curry, Somerset, three privileged tenants of the manor received two white loaves, a mess of beef and bacon with mustard, thick chicken soup, a cheese and as much ale as they could drink in the day.

Those lower in rank not only got fewer courses, but also were served smaller portions. Only the host and any exceptionally high-ranking guest got an individual serving; other high-ranking guests shared dishes (messes), usually two to a mess. If there were lower-ranking guests, as there would have been at a manor house, they were more apt to dine three or four to a mess.

In *The Manor and Manorial Records*, Nathaniel Hone recorded:

At Christmas it was frequently the custom for each tenant to give the lord a hen (partly as payment for being allowed to keep poultry) or some grain which was brewed into ale… also the lord was expected to give his tenants a meal, for example bread, cheese, pottage and two dishes of meat. The tenant might be directed to bring his own plate, mug and napkin if he wished there to be a cloth on the table, and a faggot of brushwood to cook his food, unless he wished to have it raw.

The Bishop's household, however, fared much better with almonds and raisins being bought, probably for a Christmas pudding.

The day before Christmas was kept as a fast, but a considerable amount of fish, herrings, eels and codlings were eaten, together with a salmon costing 5s 8d (28p)… On the following day (Christmas Day) even more food was consumed [by the fifteen guests, tenants and servants]. Over three days they ate no less than 1 boar, 2 complete carcasses and 3 quarters of beef, 2 calves, 4 does, 4 pigs, about 60 fowls (hens or possibly capons), 8 partridges and two geese, as well as bread and cheese. The amount of ale served was not recorded, but ten sextaries (about 40 gallons) of red wine and one of white were consumed.

Turkey and guinea-fowl were unheard of at that time, as were potatoes and many other fruit and vegetables. Hunting was a favourite pastime of Anglo-Saxon men, and the surrounding woods and meadows would have been well stocked with deer and wild boar, the primary animal represented in Yuletide customs and in Anglo-Saxon culture in general. Sheep, cattle and poultry were reared, but at Offa's Christmas feast most would have tucked into boar, venison or pork that had been roasted on a spit over the open fire. The smell would have whetted the appetites of everyone in the packed room, and great slabs of meat would be cut or torn from the carcass.

There would have been a dozen or more courses with spices and seasoning used in abundance, along with bulbs of onions and garlic to enhance the taste. Carrots, parsnips, peas and cabbage would probably have been on the menu, along with a variety of fowl. Cereals made a substantial contribution to the Anglo-Saxon diet. Wheat would be used for making bread, oats for making porridge and barley for brewing beer. Honey was used for sweetening and for brewing mead, also apples and pears for brewing cider. Herbs were widely used in the cooking, dill, thyme, opium poppy and coriander, to name just a few.

Thankfully, modern appetites have drastically decreased but there is still room for economy when it comes to over-eating at Yuletide. In fact, the health pages estimate that *everyone* puts on half a stone at Mid-Winter and a large number of people don't bother to lose it after the New Year! So with all this in mind, let's look at catering sensibly this year after a look at a *Good Housekeeping* menu that our parents and grandparents would have served ...

A Traditional Family Yuletide Feast (1955)

First Course
Scotch broth, potato or artichoke soup; or hors d'oeuvres with sardines, liver sausage, potato salad and beetroot flavoured with dried herbs

Second Course
Roast goose or 'cottage goose' (rolled, stuffed pork); or roast pheasant.

Accompaniments
Baked potatoes, buttered peas and Brussels sprouts with bacon and chestnuts.
Serve homemade preserves with pork or goose, and small

bacon-wrapped sausages with any bird.

Third Course
Plum pudding and custard sauce, flavoured with rum or brandy; or mince pies with brandy butter and sloe gin.

Dessert
Oranges, bananas, dates, figs and nuts.

Traditional fare certainly helps to simplify Yuletide catering and although one or two variations may be permissible, few families would approve of too many surprises. Whatever we choose to serve the first rule is only cook tried and tested favourites – usually limited to roast meat, two vegetables together with roast and mashed potatoes if going for the traditional meal; for ease choose a cold starter and a cold desert. To make the vegetables more interesting, try this classic Christmas side dish by livening up the Brussels sprouts by adding fried crispy bacon and boiled chestnuts; or honey-glazing the parsnips and carrots.

This isn't the time to be experimenting with all those fancy dishes to be found in the seasonal magazines because something's sure to go wrong. With wild boar back in fashion, it can make a welcome change from that American import – the turkey – as can a baked and glazed whole ham. The boar was sacred to both the Celt and the Norse people, who believed that its flesh was the food of the heroes of Valhalla, so boar, ham or pork will suffice. Serve with stuffing and 'pigs in blankets' – small sausages wrapped in streaky bacon rashers. Yuletide is a time for a bit of luxury but not everything needs to be expensive.

Nevertheless, keeping the magical symbolism in mind, this was a typical, but simple menu I'd serve in the days of those formal Mid-Winter Festival suppers:

Mid-Winter Festival Supper (1997)

Starter
Smoked salmon canapés.
Symbolising the Salmon of Wisdom or Salmon of Knowledge (*bradán feasa*), a creature figuring prominently in Celtic mythological tales, and primarily associated with wisdom and prophecy. They often inhabited the sacred wells, feeding on the fruits (often, hazelnuts) of the Tree of Life.

Main Course
Roast pork with apple sauce.
Symbolising the wild boar that was used for more than a 1,000 years to mark the festive season in this country, and the boar's head with an apple in its mouth, dates back to the Norse Yule pig sacrifice at the turn of the year.

Or:
Rib of beef with horseradish.
Symbolising the slaying of the bull is an important symbol of Mithras whose birthday falls around the Winter Solstice.
Both served with roast potatoes and parsnips, peas and carrots.

Dessert
Dried fruit compote
Cheese board
The dried fruit compote is Christmas pudding without the stodge and symbolises the fruit from the Tree of Life.

To Make
Best made a day or two ahead of the supper. Soak 1lb dried fruit (a mix of apricots, figs, raisons and sultanas, etc.,) in 10 fl oz of port and the juice of one orange. Set aside. Now drain the fruit, reserving the boozy liquor. Heat 10 fl oz of water and simmer

the dried fruit in it for 15 minutes. Remove from the heat, add the boozy liquor again and allow to cool before serving with *crème fraiche*.

This is a menu easily adapted for a single person and one I've eaten many times myself in recent years. The smoked salmon eaten is on its own with lemon, black pepper and brown bread; then either a large pork chop or a juicy steak, and half the ingredients for the dried fruit compote. Just because you've chosen to spend the festival alone doesn't mean the food can't be interesting and if we're going to spend a little more, then it's worth doing so on a small amount of something that will go a long way. There are a fabulous range of smokeries around the country so, for a Mid-Winter starter why not splurge on some perfectly smoked salmon or a selection of smoked meats to use as a starter. You *can* taste the difference.

To add variety, however, I decided to ask some of my fellow Moon Books authors what they would be likely to serve for the Mid-Winter Festival, and who was going to provide the vegetarian menu?

Elen Sentier, author of *Merlin: Once and Future Wizard, Trees of the Goddess, Elen of the Ways* and *Owl Woman* offered both:

Paul's the veggie, I came back to meat with the help of John Matthews (quite a nice vampire!). My sun-return dinner: stilton pate on sourdough toast with a really nice sherry; a hough of venison (prefer roe, but whatever) with roasties with deep fried parsnips, some of my own saved frozen peas, homemade red currant jelly with local birch wine; locally made cranberry ice cream or homemade summer pudding from my autumn hedge harvest; Lapsang or Russian Caravan tea to finish up with. Paul's veggie menu: local mushroom pate; chestnut and root veg pie with broccoli, spinach and peas; locally made brioche stuffed with my homemade whortleberry jam and served warm; coffee. And Pol Roget throughout! ... Oh and I finish up – after the tea – sipping Bruichladdich's Black Art until I become 'comfortably numb'.

Lucya Starza, author of *Candle Magic,* added:

I'm not vegetarian, although I was for about a decade from my early teens to my early 20s. My menu suggestion would actually be Polish Christmas Eve, which I have always celebrated because one side of the family is Polish. The supper has Christian symbolism, but I don't mind that as it is part of my heritage, even though I am pagan. It is also a pescetarian meal, so would suit those who eat fish, but not meat.

The meal begins with the breaking of Christmas wafers (*opłatek*). Everyone at the table breaks off a piece and eats it as a symbol of their unity with Christ. They then share a piece with each family member. A tradition exists among some families to serve twelve different dishes at *Wigilia* symbolizing the twelve apostles, or perhaps, an odd number of dishes for good luck (usually five, seven, or nine). A traditional *Wigilia* supper in Poland includes *barszcz* (beetroot soup) with *uszka* (dumplings) and fried carp. Carp provides a main component of the Christmas Eve meal across Poland; carp fillet, carp in aspic etc. Herrings are also popular as part of the meal. Universal Polish Christmas foods are *pierogi,* which are described as dumplings, but are a bit like large ravioli. They are often stuffed with potato and cheese, but you can get other fillings. For dessert, *makowiec* or noodles with poppy seeds, are common, although my family usually has poppy seed cake and gingerbread. Often there is also a compote of dry fruits.

Sheena Cundy, author of the Witch-Lit novel, *The Madness & the Magic,* said:

I celebrate Yule with my coven members (three of us) and we feast on anything really... cakes, wine, salad stuff and general 'party food'. I'm not a veggie, but I definitely struggle through Christmas every year... But our dinner menu is bog standard

I'm afraid. The usual piles of excess and left-overs! Yes, it looks like I may need this book!

Laura Perry is from the USA and author of *Ariadne's Thread*, had this to say:

We're not officially vegetarian, though we do eat vegetarian about half the time (trying to cut down on meat consumption). We celebrate on Winter Solstice, not Christmas Day, but we do pretty much the standard Christmas stuff – open presents, have a nice meal, and so on. Our typical dinner menu is not the standard one (we usually have a traditional Thanksgiving dinner with turkey and all the accessories in November since we're American, and we don't care to repeat that at Christmas). In past years, I've roasted a goose, *a la* Dickens, but in recent years our preferred menu has developed into this: Salmon Wellington (salmon plus creamed spinach in a puff pastry crust) glazed carrots, roasted cherry tomatoes with assorted pickles and relishes. Homemade dinner rolls. Cheesecake. We have a red wine, usually a Pinot Noir, with this meal.

Nimue Brown, author of *Druidry and Meditation* and *Druidry and the Ancestors* gave us something different:

My great grandmother made Christmas puddings every year in the copper boiler. This was far before my time and has passed into family myth. In my twenties, I took up pudding making, and discovered the scope to emulate her – not by popping them in the washing machine, but by making a pudding load to share with my community. It's a good way of expressing abundance and spreading cheer. I don't have an ancient and traditional Christmas pudding recipe. I mostly borrow from Delia Smith, but I use any dried fruit that takes my fancy. I put mead in it, and home-brewed wine, and they never come out the same way twice. These days, I cook them in the slow cooker, which is playing the role of both hearth and cauldron in my small flat. Puddings can get lost in the great stuffing-fest of Christmas day. They work better when sent out alone, and fed to people not already bloated. Pudding sharing – rich, tasty, extravagant, is a real joy. A pudding steaming and waiting after a cold winter walk, or brought to a social gathering gets the attention it deserves. I walked this year's a mile or so, wrapped in taped together jiffy bags to keep it hot – ancestral and contemporary magic tricks meeting in the process! For me, a pudding session is an essential part of the festive season. A stand-alone event, involving the people I love most.

Mabh Savage, author of *A Modern Celt Seeking the Ancestors* and *Celtic Witchcraft* responded with a completely different approach:

Dinner is a complex affair; my brother is a strict vegan, my mother now doesn't eat pork or dairy – the two things my six-year old craves most! My dad and I prefer poultry, but we all love our veg, which is a blessing. My dad is skilled at Indian cooking, so will spit-roast a tandoori chicken. Slightly unusual, perhaps, but absolutely delicious and goes really well with buttery mash and slightly crunchy carrots. For my brother, I go a bit mad with the veg – red cabbage cooked with garlic, stir-fried broccoli, three kinds of potatoes, herby parsnips (can't give honey to a vegan!), carefully sourced vegan gravy, plus sprouts, squash and salad. I also try to do some sort of hearty dish with lentils or chick peas, probably a *dahl*, or perhaps *chana masala*, something that fills the house from fragrant spices. Finally, for the carnivores amongst us, as well as moist chicken there are masses of pigs-in-blankets and piles of stuffing. I honestly think my little boy could live off this stuff! I rarely have puddings as I love to fill up on savoury stuff, but my other half loves panettone, so there will probably be some of this, a vegan cake courtesy of my mum who is a baking wizard, and tons of sweets and chocolate.

Martha Gray, author of *Grimalkyn: The Witch's Cat* has recently moved to California from the UK and spent her first 'Christmas' in the US.

Here the festive season traditionally begins on the fourth Thursday in November, just after the Thanksgiving holiday. On Thanksgiving Day, a spectacular parade is taken out in New York City that has the smiling figure of Santa Claus participating in it, which heralds the beginning of the Christmas shopping season. In the US, certain kinds of food are traditionally served at Thanksgiving meals. Turkey, usually roasted and stuffed (but sometimes deep-fried instead), is typically for any Thanksgiving table, so that Thanksgiving is colloquially known as 'Turkey Day'.

Around the Solstice people hold parties around the outdoor fire-pit and serve a variety of drinks, i.e. eggnog with brandy served hot in a mug, mulled wine or cider, hot toddies or mead to be drunk around the fire-pit. In addition to the meat or poultry served for dinner there are sweet potatoes with root vegetables of all kinds and Brussels sprouts (can't not have Brussels); baked pies like pumpkin, because so much is grown in the autumn to be made into pies during the Yule season together with citrus fruits, nuts, mince pies and fruitcake.

Decorations are in the reds and greens of the season with wreaths, trees, cinnamon scented pine cones and mistletoe. On my hearth I had a vase of long gold branches, evergreen leaves and branches covered with deep red berries, poinsettias and deep red flowers. Decorative bowls of dried fruit, nuts, citrus fruit, along with berries and pine cones can be placed on the hearth. Most decorations for Yule, like in the UK, can be discreetly incorporated into family celebrations without any non-pagans being any the wiser.

It's evident from our contributors, who are all committed pagans, and from different Paths and persuasions, that the Mid-Winter Festival is an important culinary occasion. In fact, so many Yuletide moments and memories are centred around food. One year my father brought home the Christmas dinner in the form of a gosling that would be fattened and eaten on the day. Needless to say, the bird became a pet and the family declared that even if it was killed, no one was going to eat it. The young bird was given to another family with the same idea in mind, but when my father asked his friend how he'd enjoyed his Christmas dinner, the reply came back: 'We finished up have a bloody chicken at the last minute because the kids wouldn't let me kill the goose!' The goose remained the family pet and watchdog until it died of old age – and what a great Mid-Winter's Tale, even if our ancestors wouldn't have approved!

The Christmas Cake

It wouldn't be Yule without the long, drawn-out ritual of the Christmas cake that starts in early December so it has time to mature, and then a fortnight later it is covered with almond paste, the icing being left until a week before Christmas. The custom is for a rich fruit cake, but many people find a plainer mixture is more enjoyable. This recipe is from a vintage Mrs Beeton's cookery book that has provided our family cake for the past 50 years without fail. Don't forget the custom of family members helping to stir the mixture and making a wish.

Ingredients
8 oz butter or margarine
8 ox castor sugar
½ teaspoon gravy browning
8 oz plain flour
¼ teaspoon salt
1 level teaspoon mixed spice
½ level teaspoon baking powder
5-6 eggs
1 lb currants
8 oz raisins
4 oz glacé cherries

2 oz chopped peel
4 ox blanched, chopped almonds
Milk, if necessary
4-5 tablespoons brandy

Line an 8-inch cake tin with greaseproof paper. Cream fat and sugar until white; add gravy browning. Sift together flour, salt mixed spice and baking powder. Add egg and flour alternately to the creamed fat, beating well between each addition. Stir in the prepared fruit, almonds and if necessary add a little milk to make a heavy dropping consistency. Place the cake mixture in the cake tin and tie a piece of paper around the outside of the tin to prevent burning. Smooth the mixture and make a depression in the centre. Bake in a warm oven (335F, 170C, Gas 3) for ½ hour then reduce heat to 290F, 150C, Gas 1 for a further 3-3½ hours. Allow to firm before removing from tin and when cold remove paper. Prick bottom of cake well and sprinkle brandy over.

The Art of 'Using-Up'

With a mother and grandmother who had to cater for a family through two world wars, I was brought up on the 'Art of Using-Up' (see *The Secret People*) and even in these days of plenty, it is an art I still practise to the present day. Of course freezing wasn't an option back then but now there is even less of an excuse for binning perfectly good food. For instance:

- Left-over sprouts and mashed potato were mixed together for 'bubble and squeak', which was traditionally served on Boxing Day with fried eggs and cold meat.
- If you have any dinner-sized portions left, box it and pop it in the freezer as 'ready meals' for one. Even the smallest amount could be pureed up for a baby, or served as a kid's portion for lunch the next day.

- Left-over roast meat can be put through the food processor to provide the base for a cottage pie. Add any left-over carrots or peas and freeze until needed. Any leftover meat should be used for making into stock for soups or gravy and frozen.

- Pick the turkey carcass clean of all the meat and freeze it in individual containers to use for curries, stir-fries, risotto, etc. You can also make a stock with the turkey bones and left-overs, which is fantastic for winter stews and soups.

- Cold sausages can be sliced and added to potato salad or mash; or seasoned and used for fillings for sandwiches or jacket potatoes.

- Ends of cheese can be grated and mixed with equal amounts of fresh cheese to use in cooked dishes such as Welsh rarebit and jacket potatoes.

- Crusts and stale bread can be blitzed in the food processor to make breadcrumbs, which can be stored in the freezer. The same can be done with cake or biscuits and used as a topping for crumbles and puddings.

- Use slices of stale bread in a bread and butter pudding, or to make breakfast 'eggy bread' by beating an egg in a bowl with seasoning. Cut slices of bread in half then dip in the egg and fry.

- The last dregs of wine or beer can be frozen in ice cube trays and popped out into stews and casseroles when cooking.

- Cut the bruises off old apples and toss into the pan with your sausages. Don't throw out those black bananas – mash them up and add cream for a super-quick pudding. Use the blitzed cake and biscuit crumbs as a topping.

And along with all the feasting comes the drinking. I can remember sideboards groaning under the weight of the booze bottles because it wasn't the done thing not to have something for everyone – guests, callers and family alike. Even Advocaat, that traditional drink made from eggs, sugar and brandy that looked like custard; the bottle was never opened and usually went down the lavatory later in the New Year. These days (hopefully) we have more sense, but it's good to have something to add to the festival spirit, so stock up on your favourite tipple, by all means! Two drinks, however, are a must:

First the hot Irish whiskey, without which, no Irish sporting activity could take place. Add a splash of boiling water to one measure of whiskey, four cloves, sugar and a slice of lemon. It *has* to be Irish whiskey, which has a smoother taste, and it is said that one can mend a broken heart – ten can cure anything! Excellent for keeping the cold at bay during the day and an effective night-cap for aiding sleep. It beats mulled wine hands down.

For those who don't drink alcohol, try to provide something other than bottled water. Available from most supermarkets, sparkling elderflower pressé is a useful drink to have around to serve chilled as a sophisticated and refreshing alternative to alcohol at any time, or for the drinkers add white wine for an aromatic spritzer. It also creates a fabulous cocktail when mixed with gin or vodka. Chilled elderflower sparkling pressé combined with pomegranate juice creates a refreshing rosé, but if you do fancy something a little stronger, add a splash of vodka. With a twist on the traditional bellini, try this 'elderflower bellini' made with a sparkling elderflower pressé and splash of peach juice – garnished with a thin peach slice and a spring of mint. Elderflower sparkling pressé poured over cranberry juice and crushed ice, and served in a long glass, looks disgustingly trendy.

For those 'doing solitary', invest in a collection of those miniature bottles of wine usually served on aircraft. It's ideal when you fancy a glass of wine with a meal, or just having a relaxing tipple by the fire in the evening without the thought of having to down a full bottle. I like prosecco, but it's not re-corkable – so last year I treated myself to a dozen small bottles and thoroughly enjoyed each one. Yes, it's a more expensive way of buying wine, but it saves on the misery of a hangover.

The Winter Solstice has been recognised as a significant turning point in the yearly cycle since the late Stone Age and those ancient megalithic sites carefully aligned with the solstice sunrise and sunset, confirm this. In reality, Mid-Winter feasting is as old as humanity itself – an ancient custom designed to break the long, dark, cold days of winter with warmth, light and revelry. It was a time of great magic and mystery and our ancestors realised this. They understood the symbolism of the short, dark days morphing into warmth and light with the return of the sun. And considering this particular pagan festival has been preserved with most of its traditions intact, it is surprising that it is too often ignored by the pagan community, frequently consigning the Winter Solstice to a minor spoke in the Wheel of the Year.

Strangely enough, it is Christianity itself that has made a mockery of 'Christmas' and turned it into the commercial free-for-all we know today. What *is* sad, is that a large number of pagans in rejecting the whole concept of Christmas are, in fact, rejecting the ancestral concept of Yule. So, lets us reclaim the Mid-Winter Festival with all its 'warmth, light and revelry' and celebrate it in time-honoured fashion *without* the commercial overtones.

Social pressures and television adverts from supermarkets and glossy magazines mean that we feel pressured into being over generous with our gift-giving and providing gargantuan meals we know we're not going to eat. Of course we want to share this bountiful cornucopia with family and friends – but why go into hock to achieve it? With a total Christmas Day food bill averaging a huge £169 per household and more than a third of the population admitting to throwing away more food at Christmas than at any other time of year, much of it could be re-used because such enormous waste is a drain on the environment as well as our personal finances. So, isn't it time that we cut the obscene amount of food waste by planning our shopping and cooking more carefully? Let's face it, most supermarkets will re-open on Boxing

Day and we are hardly going to suffer if we've eaten all the mince pies or run out of beer.

And for those who do over-indulge, there is the traditional pick-me-up that is also a comfort drink given to invalids – the posset – taken from *Traditional Witchcraft for Fields and Hedgerows.*

A Soothing Yule Posset

1 pint milk
6 fl ozs white wine
2 oz brown sugar
1 lemon
1 teaspoon ground or fresh ginger
Grating of nutmeg

Boil the milk, pour in the wine and let the mixture cool until it curdles. Strain off the curds, add the sugar, the whole lemon and spices. Serve like yoghurt.

Sometimes a New Year is seen as an opportunity to wipe the slate clean of any disappointments or perceived failures of the year just passed, or sometimes it can be seen as just another return of every other year, where we will complete the same tasks with the same people. If you are approaching this New Year with the dread that it will just be the same as every other, try to remember it is a New Year, filled with new moments that you have never been in before and filled with numerous possibilities. A few simple homilies spring to mind that are worth reflecting upon at this turning of the tide.

You can't change anything but yourself, and if you change yourself, the world changes around you.

If you wish to known of future lives, remember that your present life is a reflection of your past life.

One ought, every day at least, to hear a little song, read a good poem, see a fine picture, and, if it were possible, to speak a few reasonable words.

What we call our destiny is truly our character and that character can be altered. The knowledge that we are responsible for our actions and attitudes does not need to be discouraging, because it also means that we are free to change this destiny.

Accepting responsibility for our actions is very much a pagan ethic and this is as good a time as any to reclaim our traditions and customs – and create a few new ones into the bargain.

A Little Light Candle Magic

To find out what's in store for the future, let's see what Lucya Starza suggested in her *Pagan Portals – Candle Magic: A Witch's Guide to Spells and Rituals*, which incidentally makes an excellent Yuletide gift for any pagan friends.

One modern Pagan witchcraft tradition is to place four candles on a log during Winter Solstice celebrations, light them and watch how they burn down. Each candle represents a season of the year to come and the way it burns and shapes left by dripping wax can be used to predict what might happen in the year ahead …

Candles are lovely aids to meditation. Pretty much whatever type of meditation you choose to do, the gentle light of a candle provides the right atmosphere. You can use the flame itself as the focus for meditation. As with most types of meditation, you need to be in a restful position – seated on the floor, a cushion or a chair. Make sure the candle is positioned at eye height and is securely in its holder. Light the candle, take a few deep breaths in and out, then focus on the flame…

Because the Mid-Winter Festival is such a magical time, there are numerous opportunities for meditation and, if the circumstances permit, a candlelit vigil to see what the future holds. The best time is during the 'Between the Years' period when the tides are slack, or at Twelfth Night as the old year truly ends.

Footnote: Yuk!

The statistics for waste food over the Yuletide period is staggering – and rather stomach churning. The 'Love Food Hate Waste' campaign run by the government's waste reduction advisory body, Wrap, doesn't know whether it's because we are suckers for gluttony or incapable of calculating how much we will need to feed our family and friends for the annual Christmas feast.

Every year British households shamelessly end up chucking away a mountain of surplus festive food. We shop, we eat some of it and bin the rest. Recent figures reveal the shocking extent of our thoughtlessness. We throw out the equivalent of two million turkeys, five million Christmas puddings and a truly shocking seventy-four million mince pies. To put it into context, that means we are binning nearly twice as many mince pies as retail giant Marks & Spencer sells every year.

And if that's not bad enough, it's not just leftover turkey scraps we need to be worrying about. Britons will apparently pour fifteen *million* cups of roast turkey fat down the kitchen sink on Christmas Day, enough to nearly fill an Olympic swimming pool! Research from the University of Portsmouth has shed light on what happens to this fat once it enters sewers and transforms into a hard, soapy material. Scientists estimate removing fat, oil and grease from sewer pipes adds up to £50m a year to our household bills. *Double yuck!*

Chapter Five

The Art of Inter-Action

As poet Brendan Kennelly observed: 'Christmas is a season of contradictions. The very idea of Christmas has something contradictory about it... What is Christmas anyway? Is it the celebration of one of one of the world's most significant spiritual events? Or is it an orgy of commercialism, a cynical exploitation of the dreams of children and the end-of-year fatigue of adults?'

For the entire pagan community it *should* be one of the most sacred times of the year, but the lack of any formal written liturgy has consigned the festival to a minor observance in the pagan calendar.

Hopefully, *Have a Cool Yule* will serve its purpose in demonstrating that history *proves* the festival to be a wholly pagan event, worthy of being acknowledged as one of the great festivals of the pagan calendar along with Beltaine and Samhain. With all the different strands of pagan custom brought to the hearth-fire of the Mid-Winter Festival we all have something to celebrate in time-honoured fashion whether our ancestors are Briton, Celt, Norse or Anglo-Saxon.

Nevertheless, if we read any selection of any magazines, newspapers or colour supplements in the months leading up to Christmas, we'll find dozens of letters and articles all commenting on the problems different non-pagans face in coping with just one day in the year! The 'Christmas survival guide' features so heavily that it's obvious that even non-pagans have their misgivings about the contradictions of a traditional family Christmas!

One letter was from a fairly newly-wed who was complaining because when they got married she and her husband agreed they'd take it in turns in spending Christmas with the parents. The first year was spent with her folks and as the second year was approaching the bartering bride was trying to find ways to welch on the deal. She was even considering suggesting they went to her parents again, because 'men are generally not so sentimental about these things' and sod the in-laws' feelings! The first reaction was to wonder whether this female was above the age of consent, and the second was to open a book on how long that marriage was going to last. In Ireland a boy and his mammy aren't easily parted and the suggestion would cause ructions of epic proportion that would still be a bone of contention 20 years down the line.

Another couple were getting to boiling point because the large family always descended on the parents, but because the daughter-in-law lived locally, it always fell to her to do everything now that the mother was getting elderly. By the time Christmas Eve arrived the couple on the doorstep weren't speaking; the kids had gone into a sulk because the row had been brewing for weeks and nobody could do right. The real fly in the ointment was the old mother who kept telling the siblings that everything was 'no trouble and that *she* could manage', but with no mention made of the daughter-in-law's input. All it would have taken was a phone call and an appeal for help, instead of festering with resentment greeting the rest of the family on its arrival!

Another columnist seemed to have got it sorted with the arrangement for her to spend Christmas and Stephen's Day with her family, while he spent the time with his folks. It was their third Christmas as an unmarried couple and since they were both close to their families, they felt it was to be expected that they spend the holiday in their 'respective homeplaces'. A good idea perhaps for the unmarrieds, but what happens when (if) a marriage or move-in occurs? '*Same procedure as last year, James!*'?

For the rebellious pagan, this year might be the opportunity to 'throw a spanner in the works', 'take the bull by the horns' and 'tell the truth and shame the Devil' as my grandmother would have said. Let's face it, a family Christmas often means spending a day in the company of relatives who steadfastly refuse to show any signs of increased tolerance of your vegetarian/pagan/gay/ eccentric life-style. Despite your determination to be a) helpful and not complain regardless of fault; b) fake concern for your niece's teething problems and c) feign interest in aging relatives' political opinions – you won't be able to do right by accident either. Columnist Dr Ciara Kelly summed it up: 'People feel an inordinate amount of pressure to spend money they don't have, and to cook food they wouldn't normally eat, and to have their house look a certain way, and be cooped up amiably with people they don't get on with, and to throw a load of booze in on top and for it to all go swimmingly.'

The Art of Inter-Action, however, is another name for appeasement and one dictionary definition for this state of affairs is: 'Appeasement in a political context is a diplomatic policy of making political or material concessions to an enemy power in order to avoid conflict.' And that just about sums up the reactions should many of us dare to suggest that we might like to opt-out of the family Christmas and spend a pagan Yule in peaceful solitude. Unfortunately, parents often have a blinkered view of their offspring, their partners and the grandchildren, and see Christmas as a time for the family to get together in a spirit of love and light. This is despite the fact that siblings may have divorced from their original partners and teenage grandchildren really don't want to be bothered with new toddler cousins.

Let's Put a Stop To It... Now!

In many areas of commerce and business, the Mid-Winter break has now been extended to include the whole week from Christmas Eve up to the New Year Bank Holiday, which puts increasing pressure on people to spend more time where they don't want to be. So, the ideal solution is to tell the family well in advance that you'll be spending 'the Day' in your own home, and arrange other days, such as Mother's Night, Boxing Day or New Year's Day, to visit with family. The news might be as welcome as a Jesuit's sermon at a Beltaine Bash, but in the long term it will take all the stress out of deciding who's going where for Yuletide. Stay at home and start to build your own traditions around what should be a precious and magical time for *everyone* regardless of faith, belief or denomination.

At the other end of the spectrum, we do have the question of loneliness, which can often strike with a vengeance at Yuletide – and it *is* possible to feel lonely in a house full of people with whom you feel you have nothing in common. This is something you need to sort out by yourself and make the effort to get out and connect with other people in similar circumstances. After all, the Mid-Winter Festival is all about having fun and it is possible to extend the party season for the whole of those thirty-two days of Yule if you have the stamina. Nevertheless, hosting the Mid-Winter Festival celebration under your own terms is the greatest compliment you can pay your fellow pagans. Don't be afraid to try something different... just make sure the bathroom cabinet is well-stocked with Gaviscon and Alka-Seltza.

Of course, not all families are anti-pagan and it may be that you want to try to combine the two approaches to the holiday season. After all, the ancient Britons thought the fire festivals of the Celts were a good idea, and the introduction of the Norse Yule found favour with the Anglo-Saxons. By amalgamating these customs and cultures our pagan forebears found themselves in the same position as modern Christians who often share symbolism with another faith. Chanukah, the Jewish eight-day, wintertime 'festival of lights', is celebrated with a nightly menorah lighting, special prayers and fried foods; the menorah holds nine flames, one of which is the *shamash* ('attendant'), which is used to kindle the other eight lights. On the first night, just one flame is lit; on the second night an additional flame is lit and by the eighth night of Chanukah, all eight lights are kindled. A menorah is lit in every Jewish household and placed in a window – and thousands of people believe this distinctive candle-holder to be a Christmas decoration often fuelled by electricity!

Compromise – rather than appeasement – is the way to make the Yuletide celebrations go with a swing and still manages to keep those important family members happy. Rather than turning our backs on Christmas entirely, perhaps we should try to implement a few ideas of our own to help things along. Habits *do* change over the years as older members of the family die and it may be that your parents and siblings are bored rigid by the habitual routine that was implemented during their parents' day. Suggest a family Yule at your home so that you retain control over the festivities and keep it to just one day; introduce a few subtle changes so that although people are aware of the differences, there's not enough to make it unfamiliar or uncomfortable.

Things to Do at Yuletide

A candle-lit door entrance creates a wonderfully welcoming look to greet your guests during the festive season. So back to the garden centre for those large outside storm lanterns or hurricane lamps; I got mine for under £10 from the supermarket, and they make highly acceptable Yuletide gifts, too. Use a mix of pink and ivory candles with the lanterns draped with pink ribbons and ivy to create a festive look – and if you live on the road-side make sure the local yobos can't make off with them to give to *their* mothers for Xmas! Or the local dogs can't use them as a peeing-post. Unless you have a covered entrance porch, place them just inside the door in the hall or at the bottom of the stairs.

Mid-Winter entertaining is all about atmosphere and ambiance, so put plenty of thought into your arrangements, especially if catering for different ages. Beg, borrow or buy a selection of family films that appeal to most age groups – those without gratuitous bad language, sex or violence – and if you can prise the younger generation away from their phones and iPads for a while, suggest they join you in taking the dog for a walk to catch up on the gossip. After all, it's just for one day and the dog will probably need to exercise, too.

Playing games is often viewed as being *passé*, but once you coax everyone to take part it's surprising just how much all the generations can enjoy them if they're not required to do anything that makes them appear foolish. My grandmother cut through any objections by saving all her 'copper' (low denomination coins) throughout the year and giving everyone a 'stake' to play with. There were two games that kept everyone entertained throughout Christmas Night ...

Put and Take

Put and take was a game that first became known during the First World War (1914-18). The full history of the game is unclear, but it was thought to have been invented by a soldier in the trenches. The original game was made from a brass bullet that the soldier had shaped into a spinning top with six sides. Each side had an instruction on that was either Put one, Put two, Put all, Take one ,Take two, or Take all. The top was spun by players, who each put an ante in the pot (said to be a cigarette), and depending on how the top fell either took or put how many cigarettes indicated. The game became so popular that during the 1920-30s it was introduced as a gambling game, predominantly played in the North of England in working men's clubs and pubs. Because the top would virtually last forever, being made of brass, the commercial production of Put and Take did not last for long and during the next 40 years the playing of the game gradually died out. Replicas can now be purchased from e-Bay.

Rules:
Any number of players can play. Each player puts a coin or in the pot.
The first player spins the top. If the top come down 'Put' side uppermost the player puts into the pot the amount indicated (i.e. Put one, two or all).

For 'Put all' the player doubles the amount in the pot. If the spinner lands with 'Take' side uppermost the player takes the amount indicated from the pot.

For 'Take all' the player takes the whole pot.

Each player puts a coin in the pot and the next player spins and the game goes on until somebody spins 'Take all' and the game is re-started.

Newmarket

This game is perfect for anyone feeling nostalgic about spending countless Christmas nights with family members getting excited at the prospect of winning a few pence. To take a trip down memory lane, take the Jack of Spades, Queen of Diamonds, King of Clubs and Ace of Hearts out of one deck and place them in a square in the middle of the table with a gap in between for the kitty. These are the 'horses'.

Each player places a penny in the kitty, plus an additional stake on the card of his or her choice. Each person takes it in turns to deal, and the entire second pack is dealt out between the players, plus an extra 'dummy' hand. Ace is either high or low. The player to the left of the dealer opens with their lowest card – say, two of diamonds – to be followed by the three, four and five until the run stops because the dummy hand prevents the run from being completed.

The person playing the last card in a sequence, must begin a new run with their lowest card in a suit of another colour. The first person to empty their hand takes the kitty, and if at any time someone plays the Jack, Queen, King or Ace, they collect whatever amount is on that card. If the kitty remains uncollected when someone goes out, it carries over to the next game.

Trivia Games

More serious gatherings can be kept amused with Trivial Pursuit or other trivia board games or quizzes, especially if you prevent the dunces in the party from feeling left out by making it a team game. Depending on the number of guests there can be two, three or four teams and each team leader takes it in turn to select the members for his or her team. My mother was always a popular choice because she was a demon on sports subjects, particularly football, while others of her generation rarely answered a question. Even the thickest cousin can be included and everyone enjoys being part of the team that was declared the winner.

Would I Lie to You?

This popular television game show can easily be adapted for a fun Christmas night or New Year's Eve party and it's better than Who Am I? – where the younger members of the family select obscure celebrities no one has ever heard of – or Charades, where some folk try to be too clever for their own good. Write a series of life-style scenarios on cards and each player has to select one without looking at it…then reads out his or her claim such as: 'I once spent the night locked in the London Dungeon' or 'I was once bitten by a rabid bat'. Then comes the what, why, when, where and how series of questions followed by a vote as to whether it's a truth or lie. The winner can either be the most convincing or, if it's played as a team game, the ones who lie the best!

Other Games

To see if it was possible to add to my selection, I browsed the internet and came up with 'Nine Must-Have Christmas Party Games for Adults' because let's face it, there's usually not much to do at a usual family gathering, other than get drunk or talk. These *adult* suggestions involved stuffing balloons into nylon tights, stomping on balloons, a drawing competition, a guessing game, singing, picking up items with chopsticks, guessing the contents of a sock, a drinking game and dressing up! Now I don't know about you, but I loathe the sort of games that insult my intelligence and I can't think of anyone among my friends who would gladly participate in this kind of nonsense. And if people are made to feel self-conscious, stupid or embarrassed then the party is *not* going to go with a swing. Admittedly I'm not much of a team-player so I can quite cheerfully spend my Yuletide *sans* party games, but looking back at those modest gambling we used to enjoy, and some that I've been forced to participate in during later years, I must say the old ones are still the best for getting everyone together.

All I can say is: try it! If you've attempted to bridge the divide and it fails, then it's not your fault and the family only have themselves to blame if you inform them that next year you really are opting out!

Other Things to Think About

Yuletide isn't the time to get stressed out by future plans and New Year resolutions, but as Twelfth Night approaches, it might be a good idea to put a couple of life-style improvements into operation.

- First on the list, of course, is getting our finances in order. Hopefully, we've had the most frugal Yuletide ever…and still managed to enjoy it! An idea that won't break the bank is the start of a rainy-day fund for unexpected events or emergencies. Most of us these days bank online, so it is easy to transfer a small amount each week/month into a savings account; or if you're not into online banking, invest in one of those large money tins that have to be opened with a tin-opener. Drop all your loose change into it every evening and you'll be surprised how it will soon amount up – you can even use it to save for next Yule!
- Sleeping better means realising that what we do during the day can have an impact on how we sleep at night: so things like regular meal times, avoiding exercising late at night, keeping caffeine levels to a minimum all help sleep. Wind-down time is really important, so about an hour and a half before bedtime we should reduce all work activities (i.e.

switch off the computer) to prepare the body and mind for sleep. Don't use alcohol as a sleep aid and don't eat too late at night. The bedroom should be kept as dark as possible, which helps with melatonin levels – a *natural* hormone that is produced by the pineal gland in humans and animals, regulating sleep and wakefulness. This is what is now called 'sleep hygiene' and these things are what we should all be doing to get a good night's rest.

- The reason why most of us don't stick to our New Year's resolutions is because we lack the enthusiasm for the target we set ourselves. If we make our goals tangible and something that we'll look forward to achieving, we stand more chance of achieving them. Work out how you're going to reach that goal and then set out to make small, gradual changes because we can't make drastic changes to our lifestyle overnight.

- Whatever that goal may be, it can be frustrating when it doesn't come to fruition immediately. So allow yourself time. Remember that life is a journey, not a destination, so don't wait until you get where you want to be to allow yourself to feel happy. Enjoy the process of the travelling.

- When we get stuck in a rut, we usually end up staying at home most of the time, missing out on a lot of interesting opportunities. Meeting new people can be beneficial to our mental well-being, so don't be afraid to get out there and make some new friends. Also spend more time with the people that matter because there's just too little time in this life for us to waste it on insincere, duplicitous and toxic company. We should focus on the people who we care about deeply and who care about us, as this is the best way to stay happy.

- Expand the mind and learn more about art, music, culture etc. Topics like this often confuse people, but they can be enjoyable if we spend enough time learning about them and spend less time on social media. It's fine to stay in touch with friends and family, but if you consistently spend more than an hour every day on social media, it's time to stop because this has become a serious addiction among a wide range of adults. Instead, enhance your magical and mystical awareness through the exploration of the wealth of universal memories of myth, fantasy and symbolism concealed within these various artistic mediums.

- Lastly, it might also be a good idea to make a concerted effort to understand more about the ancestral elements of your pagan lifestyle, since it was necessary for you to turn to this book in the first place! The people who make the most noise on the internet are those who like to pontificate about what is, and what isn't the 'real' pagan ethos. A pagan life-style is more than caring for the planet and becoming vegetarian. It is honouring and respecting the ancient pagan traditions and doing everything in our power to maintain them.

Even if our life is going swimmingly, there is always room for improving our life-style and perception of life. There are a lot of pagan platitudes that extol the virtues of taking offence on behalf of others, but spirituality doesn't necessarily refer to religion or believing in anything particular, it can mean a basic empathy with the planet – doing what we *need* to do to make ourselves happy, instead of worrying about what everyone else thinks or needs. Checking in with our own priorities on a regular basis is a sure fire way of asking ourselves what's truly important in life.

So organising our plans for having a Cool Yule is one of the first steps towards claiming back our pagan life-style, but doesn't mean upsetting folk or causing a family rift in order to assert our pagan independence. If they're truthful, the majority of people probably like the thought of being at home for Yuletide and it's their own personal prejudices that get in the way. They see participating in the festivities as some sort of betrayal of their pagan principals, but this should not be the case. Handled correctly we can make sure we reap the benefits of both worlds.

To sum it all up, I liked these comments from Lucya Starza:

> The truth is, I love Christmas/Yule/Winter Solstice/Winter Holidays or whatever anyone likes to call it. I happily to go carol services as well as pagan rituals. I go to the pantomime with about twenty other adults who go every year; I go to tree-dressing parties and I have friends over for Twelfth Night games. I'm a total tart when it comes to the festive season. Oh, and I do celebrate my name day: St Lucy's Day, on December 13th. There are some suggestions that although this is a saint's day, it originally celebrated a pagan goddess of light who brought light into the homes during the darkest days...

And from Mabh Savage:

> Despite being a Pagan, I do celebrate Christmas. This is down to tradition really, as my parents didn't want me to be excluded from Christmas fun (despite being Pagan themselves), so since being small, Christmas has always been a time of anticipation and wonder, and the food is my favourite part! I adore getting friends and family together for a great feast, to bond, stay warm, and to remember times before fridges and freezers, when all the perishables needed to be eaten so they wouldn't rot.

So, perhaps we all should literally take a leaf or two out of Lucya's and Mabh's books, and while sticking to our personal rules and regulations concerning gift-giving and feasting, we can still reclaim the pagan Mid-Winter Festival as our own. This doesn't mean sitting sour-faced on the side-lines, but celebrating the ancient magic and mystery by throwing ourselves whole-heartedly into the revels.

Remember, the majority of supposedly 'Christian' superstitions and traditions we observe today *are* from our pagan past and they probably wouldn't have been preserved down through the ages if all those different Briton, Roman, Celtic, Norse and Anglo-Saxon strands hadn't melded successfully together. When we sit down to our Mid-Winter Festival dinner on December 25th, regardless of whether we're part of a family gathering or spending it alone, we are participating in a ritual that stretches back to the very dawn of humanity.

About the Author

Mélusine Draco's highly individualistic teaching methods and writing draw on historical sources supported by academic texts and current archaeological findings; endorsing the view that magic is an amalgam of science and art, and that magic is the outer route to the inner Mysteries. She is the author of several titles currently published with John Hunt Publishing including the best-selling six-part Traditional Witchcraft series; two titles on power animals – *Aubry's Dog* and *Black Horse, White Horse*; *By Spellbook & Candle: Cursing, Hexing, Bottling and Binding*; *By Wolfsbane and Mandrake Root: The Shadow World of Plants and Their Poisons*; *The Secret People*; *Pan: Dark Lord of the Forest*; *The Dictionary of Magic & Mystery* published by Moon Books; *Magic Crystals Sacred Stones* and *The Atum-Re Revival* published by Axis Mundi Books.

Website:
http://www.covenofthescales.com
Website:
http://www.templeofkhem.com
Blog:
http://melusinedracoattempleofkhem.blogspot.com/
Facebook:
https://www.facebook.com/Melusine-Draco-486677478165958
Facebook:
http://www.facebook.com/TradBritOldCraft
Facebook:
http:// www.facebook.com/TempleofKhem
Facebook:
http://www.facebook.com/TempleHouseArchive

We think you will also enjoy…

Candle Magic, Lucya Starza

Using candles in simple spells, seasonal rituals and essential craft
techniques.

*…a comprehensive guide on how to use candles for spells,
in rituals and for meditation and divination. It has quickly
become my preferred book for all aspects of candle magic.*
Philip Heselton

978-1-78535-043-6 (Paperback)
978-1-78535-044-3 (e-book)

Best Selling Pagan Portals & Shaman Pathways

Celtic Chakras, Elen Sentier

Tread the British native shaman's path, explore the Goddess
hidden in the ancient stories; walk the Celtic chakra spiral
labyrinth.

*Rich with personal vision, the book is an interesting exploration of
wholeness*
Emma Restall Orr

978-1-78099-506-9 (paperback)
978-1-78099-507-6 (e-book)

Best Selling Pagan Portals & Shaman Pathways

Druid Shaman, Danu Forest

A practical guide to Celtic shamanism with exercises and
techniques as well as traditional lore for exploring the Celtic
Otherworld

A sound, practical introduction to a complex and wide-ranging subject
Philip Shallcrass

978-1-78099-615-8 (paperback)
978-1-78099-616-5 (e-book)

Kitchen Witchcraft, Rachel Patterson
Take a glimpse at the workings of a Kitchen Witch and share in
the crafts

*A wonderful little book which will get anyone started on Kitchen
Witchery. Informative, and easy to follow*
Janet Farrar & Gavin Bone

978-1-78099-843-5 (paperback)
978-1-78099-842-8 (e-book)

Moon Magic, Rachel Patterson
An introduction to working with the phases of the Moon

...a delightful treasury of lore and spiritual musings that should be essential to any planetary magic-worker's reading list.
David Salisbury

978-1-78279-281-9 (paperback)
978-1-78279-282-6 (e-book)

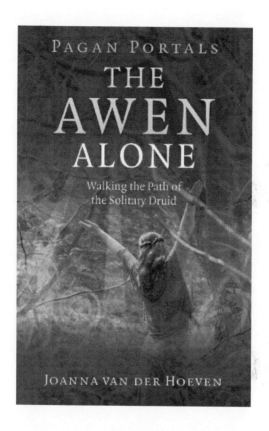

The Awen Alone, Joanna van der Hoeven
An introductory guide for the solitary Druid

Joanna's voice carries the impact and knowledge of the ancestors,
combined with the wisdom of contemporary understanding.
Cat Treadwell

978-1-78279-547-6 (paperback)
978-1-78279-546-9 (e-book)

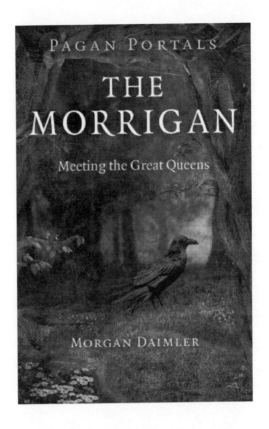

The Morrigan, Morgan Daimler

On shadowed wings and in raven's call, meet the ancient Irish
Goddess of war, battle, prophecy, death, sovereignty, and magic

*...a well-researched and heartfelt guide to the Morrigan from a fellow
devotee and priestess*
Stephanie Woodfield

978-1-78279-833-0 (paperback)
978-1-78279-834-7 (e-book)

MOON BOOKS

PAGANISM & SHAMANISM

What is Paganism? A religion, a spirituality, an alternative belief system, nature worship? You can find support for all these definitions (and many more) in dictionaries, encyclopaedias, and text books of religion, but subscribe to any one and the truth will evade you. Above all Paganism is a creative pursuit, an encounter with reality, an exploration of meaning and an expression of the soul. Druids, Heathens, Wiccans and others, all contribute their insights and literary riches to the Pagan tradition. Moon Books invites you to begin or to deepen your own encounter, right here, right now.

If you have enjoyed this book, why not tell other readers by posting a review on your preferred book site. Recent bestsellers from Moon Books are:

Journey to the Dark Goddess
How to Return to Your Soul
Jane Meredith
Discover the powerful secrets of the Dark Goddess and transform your depression, grief and pain into healing and integration.
Paperback: 978-1-84694-677-6 ebook: 978-1-78099-223-5

Shamanic Reiki
Expanded Ways of Working with Universal Life Force Energy
Llyn Roberts, Robert Levy
Shamanism and Reiki are each powerful ways of healing; together,
their power multiplies. *Shamanic Reiki* introduces techniques to
help healers and Reiki practitioners tap ancient healing wisdom.
Paperback: 978-1-84694-037-8 ebook: 978-1-84694-650-9

Pagan Portals – The Awen Alone
Walking the Path of the Solitary Druid
Joanna van der Hoeven
An introductory guide for the solitary Druid, *The Awen Alone* will
accompany you as you explore, and seek out your own place
within the natural world.
Paperback: 978-1-78279-547-6 ebook: 978-1-78279-546-9

A Kitchen Witch's World of Magical Herbs & Plants
Rachel Patterson
A journey into the magical world of herbs and plants, filled with
magical uses, folklore, history and practical magic. By popular
writer, blogger and kitchen witch, Tansy Firedragon.
Paperback: 978-1-78279-621-3 ebook: 978-1-78279-620-6

Medicine for the Soul
The Complete Book of Shamanic Healing
Ross Heaven
All you will ever need to know about shamanic healing and how to
become your own shaman…
Paperback: 978-1-78099-419-2 ebook: 978-1-78099-420-8

Shaman Pathways – The Druid Shaman
Exploring the Celtic Otherworld
Danu Forest
A practical guide to Celtic shamanism with exercises and techniques as well as traditional lore for exploring the Celtic Otherworld.
Paperback: 978-1-78099-615-8 ebook: 978-1-78099-616-5

Traditional Witchcraft for the Woods and Forests
A Witch's Guide to the Woodland with Guided Meditations and Pathworking
Melusine Draco
A Witch's guide to walking alone in the woods, with guided meditations and pathworking.
Paperback: 978-1-84694-803-9 ebook: 978-1-84694-804-6

Wild Earth, Wild Soul
A Manual for an Ecstatic Culture
Bill Pfeiffer
Imagine a nature-based culture so alive and so connected, spreading like wildfire. This book is the first flame…
Paperback: 978-1-78099-187-0 ebook: 978-1-78099-188-7

Naming the Goddess
Trevor Greenfield
Naming the Goddess is written by over eighty adherents and scholars of Goddess and Goddess Spirituality.
Paperback: 978-1-78279-476-9 ebook: 978-1-78279-475-2

Shapeshifting into Higher Consciousness
Heal and Transform Yourself and Our World with Ancient
Shamanic and Modern Methods
Llyn Roberts
Ancient and modern methods that you can use every day to
transform yourself and make a positive difference in the world.
Paperback: 978-1-84694-843-5 ebook: 978-1-84694-844-2

Readers of ebooks can buy or view any of these bestsellers by
clicking on the live link in the title. Most titles are published in
paperback and as an ebook. Paperbacks are available in traditional
bookshops. Both print and ebook formats are available online.

Find more titles and sign up to our readers' newsletter at
http://www.johnhuntpublishing.com/paganism
Follow us on Facebook at https://www.facebook.com/MoonBooks
and Twitter at https://twitter.com/MoonBooksJHP